Moved by MeToo
Owning Up and Reaching Out

Tom Bissonette

Moved by MeToo – Owning Up and Reaching Out

ISBN 978-0-359-43346-9

Dedication

To those, who through their sexual shame, have suffered and brought suffering on others.

In other words, just about all of us.

The list of those who contributed to this book is long, but they are members of a distinguished club. They have all left imprints of both joy and pain on my heart.

Some are women who allowed me to be close to them, physically, and sometimes close emotionally as well. Those I have loved earned their membership through staying in my life and/or mind long enough to establish permanent residence.

Those I have hurt paid the tuition for some of my life lessons. I am deeply indebted to them and hope they benefitted in some way, and I pray that their pain was brief and forgettable.

Mostly, I thank my mother. She had a brilliant mind and a tormented soul. She raised eight children into functioning adults at great cost to her identity and personal fulfillment. She was two-spirited; a woman who yearned for freedom and excitement, and a wife and mother imprisoned in domestic life. Through her sorrow I learned the importance of caring for others without neglecting myself.

Acknowledgements

Several people helped me improve this book with their honest but mostly gentle critiques.

Thanks to Jane Bissonette for her laser sharp proofreading skills and her suggestions about content.

Ed Smith and Sherry Hamby were generous with their recommendations about organizing the book and improving the style.

Kathy Spake and Mary Ellen Pearsall offered encouragement with their scrutiny and positive feedback.

Hilary and Justin Evans were the first who insisted I change the title if I wanted to get more people interested. The original title was "Saving Skinned Rabbit - Reflections on the MeToo Era" You'll have to read further to figure out why I chose that initially.

Warning: If you are unable to see the MeToo movement as a possible opportunity to grow, then I suggest you don't buy this book. It might make your head explode!

Foreword

In just a few years since my earlier book, <u>Sexual Civility</u>, I have learned much by immersing myself in discussions and research on current sexual and gender issues. The emergence of the MeToo movement has energized my sense of urgency about gender and sexual justice. It has also given rise to fears that people will reject the idea behind the movement because they believe it's about women vs. men, and that men will be harmed by it. Nothing could be less true.

I cannot and would not try to speak for the MeToo movement nor can I speak for other men. I can, however, address these issues as a person, a psychotherapist, and as an expert on adolescent and young adult development.

Both men and women can benefit from coming to terms with our societal neurosis about sexuality, and the cruelty often inflicted by us, intentional or otherwise. Besides being an opportunity for women to speak out and hold men accountable, the MeToo movement presents a chance for men to experience an awakening. Fears that men will be victims of false accusations are occasionally warranted but exaggerating them only serves to block the advancement of justice. Anxiety about change is normal but it's a necessary condition in the improvement of society. We must be vigilant in recognizing and thwarting political forces that attempt to divide men and women.

To make the point that sometimes men and women unknowingly hurt each other, this book is much more auto-biographical than my earlier books. In this book, I will be "owning my shit." After reading it, I hope other people will step forward and do the same. Only by sharing our past mistakes and lessons learned can we begin to heal as a nation. Although many women and men have been rattled by MeToo, many of us have been moved to conduct serious self-examination. I'm reminded of an updated version of the old saying, "The truth will set you free, but first, it will hurt like hell." It does, and it will.

To amplify my take on these issues, I include anecdotes about friends and some individuals I have talked with professionally (all anonymous). Mostly, I am offering up many of my own life experiences (not anonymous) in the hope of helping other men understand themselves, and to understand why so many women are frustrated with us. Obviously, women would be upset at those who directly mistreated them, but all of us are complicit in some way. Just being one of the "good guys" is not enough. Launching counter-campaigns like "HimToo" are false equivalents because unfounded accusations are nowhere near on the same scale as sexual assaults in frequency, and because sexually assaulting someone is more damaging than lying about them. Sticks and stones vs. words.

As a younger man, I became incarcerated by my own sense of privilege and entitlement. I did some things I regret but I understand why I did them. Like any group who gains power and privilege, we are wary of giving it up, even if it's good for us to do so. This was a struggle for me and it's a struggle that doesn't end with an epiphany or two.

The freedom offered by losing privileged status is unnerving, but it IS freedom. Not having to conform to rigid gender roles is liberating, but it takes getting used to. We forget that these roles were created for us whether they suited us or not. Traditional gender roles also restrict our beliefs about sexual norms and this creates unnecessary angst around physical attractiveness and performance issues. These norms, intended to be comforting guides to expected behavior, end up making us uncomfortable with who we are.

To move forward, those of all sex and gender identities must realize that human sexuality is a powerful force that people must harness for mutual benefit. It's like breaking a wild horse without breaking its spirit. It takes practice, patience, and humility. The horse is stronger than we are, but WE can be smarter. Intelligent sex is the best kind because it maximizes the pleasure we receive now and minimizes any pain we might feel later. It also allows us to know when to keep the figurative "horse in the barn."

Even if you consider yourself asexual, you live in a sexual world and it behooves you to understand the dynamics of this complex set of behaviors. As I stated in Sexual Civility, for lots of reasons many people are not fully present when they engage in sexual activity. As I explained then, "My aim is to help people be more aware of internal and external influences that produce a hypnotic state that clouds their judgment and diminishes their human experience."

Sex, after all, is not just an activity; it's an interpersonal process. Each sexual encounter has meaning. Often the meaning is different for each partner. This can be most harmful when we are unaware of, or don't disclose our real motivations. Sadly, sometimes life-altering decisions are made in the foggy atmosphere of sexual trance, self-deception, or shameful lies.

As another part of this endeavor I will continue to make the case that rigid gender and sex roles are contrary to real intimacy and no longer optimize survival for most of us. This includes my idea that traditional romance as a means of human coupling must be replaced by something more straightforward and functional - given the demands of modern living. Basing a relationship on feeding each other's narcissism with romantic gestures sets up unrealistic expectations. When the honeymoon is over, and the magic disappears, we are left with a real person, the person we should have gotten to know in the beginning.

Perhaps even more important, people should have the freedom to be who they want to be every day without the unnecessary constraints of some role expectations. This is not just because it's the right thing or the fair thing; it's about adaptation and survival. Couples and other social units who can switch roles or modify them to meet changing circumstances have an edge. For most of us, compatibility is no longer based on gender templates, it's based on the capacity to understand, negotiate, and compromise.

The ideas presented here have implications for our social, educational, legal, and economic systems. With social and economic change happening at lightning speed, educators and other adult guides are quickly inheriting more responsibility to teach young people how to prepare themselves for a future that demands precise communication and inter-personal role flexibility. Further, a new and deeper kind of intimacy is needed to make contemporary relationships more viable and enjoyable.

Although the main topics of this book are sex and relationships, the theme is redemption – mine and that of others. I'm not claiming special moral status or special knowledge that will have universal appeal. In fact, in some ways I have been a very slow learner. It has taken me a lifetime to figure out what some people seem to know by their mid-twenties. I'm simply sharing my views, on sex, relationships, and happiness, in the hope this will inspire more open conversations between men and women and those of all genders. We CAN understand and help one another if we create a common language and we want it bad enough.

Table of Contents

One - The Innocence Beam and the Shame Shadow

"I'm interested in how innocence fares when it collides with hard reality." - Geoffrey S. Fletcher

How It Began

Although this book is more of an analysis of the issues surrounding the MeToo phenomenon than an historical account, it's important to remember how the movement started. In 2006 Tarana Burke, a social activist used the phrase "Me Too" to promote awareness of women of color experiencing sexual abuse. She had met a teen victim and was at a loss regarding what to say. Later she wished she had simply said "me too."

In 2017 Alyssa Milano encouraged the use of MeToo with the hashtag after accusations were made against Harvey Weinstein. By the end of the first day #MeToo had been used over two hundred thousand times. It increased exponentially from there. This explosion of people going public with their stories about sexual harassment and assault made it clearer that as a society we needed to address the issues.

Backlash was fierce as many people saw this as a threat and attempted to frame the MeToo movement as an overreaction by men-hating feminists or troubled woman. Nonetheless, the movement has put the spotlight on the issue of sexual assault as never before.

My reflections on this movement are just that, only reflections. While I take strong positions and propose solutions, it will take many people acting in good faith to solve these complex problems and make the world a safer space for potential victims, and a better place for all of us to find relational fulfillment free of abuse.

So, for a better understanding of the movement itself there are better sources than this book. However, if you want to take a deep dive into potential causes and solutions of sexual misconduct and relationship problems, you're in the right place. If you work in the field of education, psychology, health services, legal services, or law enforcement this is book offers rich food for thought.

The Innocence Beam

As a psychotherapist and as a person I have spent a lifetime attempting to decipher the inner workings of the human psyche and sought to understand the resulting behavior. I've seen the best and worst of people, including myself. I live by the code that everyone does the best they can with what they have (at the time). I believe that there is positive intent in all human actions. Everything we do is either aimed at seeking/giving pleasure, or intended to reduce our own suffering or discomfort, or that of others. When we put our own needs too far above others' needs we are at our worst. When we put others needs too far above our own, we are at our highest vulnerability.

We are born with an innocence beam that shines brightly on our experiences when they are happening. Except for a relatively few natural-born psychopaths among us, we default to a state of innocence. Even our legal system reflects this in declaring us "innocent until proven guilty." I would paraphrase this as it applies to life in general as, "We are innocent until we become our guilt."

Many great thinkers have grappled with definitions of the word guilt and have tried to differentiate it from shame. For the purpose of this book, guilt is an awareness of one's wrongdoing, while shame is feeling that something is wrong with oneself. Shame is "becoming our guilt."

Shame is taught by our caregivers and others we encounter when we are children, mostly by the way they react to our innate need to explore our world. Harshness and cruelty are infectious and there is no vaccine for this disease. Prevention is possible but difficult, and we are just beginning to find effective ways to stop it before it starts. Cruelty, however, has a cause and a cure and hopefully this book can be part of your remedy.

I approach this task with the awareness that I'm sharing stories about others without judgement and trying to apply the same standard to myself. One author is a version of me, sitting in my comfortable recliner, objectively analyzing friends and people I've seen professionally. The other author is a different version of me, sitting on a hard slab, trying to make sense of my own actions and mistakes. Both authors are also witness to human triumphs, which will be gleefully shared. But first – some contrasting stories of innocence, longing to proclaim its wonder.

Like a Virgin

When a friend of mine was a teen he and a girl of the same age were outdoors on a blanket having sex for the first time. After some clumsy foreplay, they started intercourse and after a minute or two, she asked him to stop. He complied with her urgent request and she started to cry. He held her in his arms as she forced a question through her sobs, "Am I still a virgin?"

He didn't know how to answer this since he had not studied the esoteric science of Virginology, so he began looking on the blanket for some kind of tangible evidence. Finding none, he assured her that she was, indeed, still a virgin.

Hers and His

Another friend told me that she was hiding in her bedroom closet exploring her body by age eight. She soon graduated to more deliberate masturbating and finally reached her first climax at age ten. She never discussed this with anyone even though she had the habit of confessing virtually everything she did.

If she did something wrong at school, or while out playing with friends, she couldn't wait to tell a parent, usually her father who was less strict. Some days she couldn't wait for him to come home from work, so she could climb up into his lap and recite her litany of sins. But there was something about masturbation that made her feel something different from guilt, something she must carry on her own. Is it as simple as an instinct found in other mammals that sex in the open makes us vulnerable to attack? Perhaps she was observed touching herself in public and was told, "Don't do that."

A couple told me their thirteen-year-old boy masturbated to completion for the first time. He came out of his room and found his parents who were watching TV and he proudly announced, "Mom, Dad, I ejaculated!" They were pleased that he felt comfortable telling them, but his dad said, "That's wonderful, son, but you probably shouldn't announce it to your class at school tomorrow."

The Greatest Sin

One of my clients, a man in his thirties was going through a divorce. He married when he impregnated his girlfriend when they were both in their early twenties. He told me he didn't really want to marry her, but he felt it was his duty. I asked him why they did not use birth control at the time the pregnancy occurred. He answered, "I was raised in a family that believed that sex was dirty and premarital sex was even worse. The ultimate crime, however, was 'premeditated' sex. If I had planned for it I would be guilty of sex in the first degree!"

Clandestine Polyamory

The-above subtitle is a contradiction in terms. Polyamory involves a loving relationship wherein three or more people share love with each other. Aside from the fact that it could be complicated, it at least attempts to be open and honest. A client of mine had a live-in boyfriend and a female lover. She had managed to maintain both relationships for over a year without either knowing about the other.

She came to therapy and asked me how she could continue this love arrangement free of stress, especially with the pressures of school, etc. She was not bothered by sex outside marriage or having a lesbian relationship per se, nor was I concerned about those factors. She basically was asking for help with time management. She had almost been caught with the girl friend because she tried to cram too much into one day.

This presented an ethical dilemma for me because I felt uncomfortable with the idea that I would be a party to helping her do a better job at keeping her secrets. I wanted to support her, and even tried to rationalize that maybe a "don't ask, don't tell" kind of situation was not as bad as lying. Then it dawned on me that even the answer to a simple question like "Where are you going?" would necessitate an occasional lie. Her preferred plan was unrealistic.

I ended up telling her I could help her manage her time better, but I was concerned about the deception piece. She asked to see a different counselor in our office and said she just wouldn't tell them about her relationships and she asked me not to divulge it either. It was then I realized that it wasn't the sex that had a hold on her, or the love she couldn't give up; it was the sneaking and lying that excited her. She was acting out her father's history of "running around." Our shame is often rooted in or early experiences.

My Early Years

I was born surrounded by "girls", my three older sisters, a mother, and a grandmother. My father was essentially absent. He was mostly working to support us since our mom stayed at home. The rest of the time he was drinking. My mother was at best indifferent to me, sometimes even cold.

She did her "duty" as a traditional mother, cooking and cleaning, but it didn't seem like a labor of love, more like a sentence to hard labor for life. Eventually she bore eight children and did the best she could to meet our needs. She was intelligent and well-read despite leaving school in the seventh grade. She married my father when she was sixteen. She was a tormented soul, but fundamentally a good and courageous person. She was a bold feminist at heart, but she was terrified of the world. In retrospect, she was suffering from untreated depression and severe social anxiety. Despite her occasional neglect and abuse, I bear no grudge and I now marvel at how she could accomplish as much as she did.

The only time I recall her holding me was when I was eight or nine, right after I split my head open playing tag. I had tripped on an exposed tree root and took a header into a stack of bricks. She held me while my grandmother fetched some cold water and a clean wash cloth. When the water arrived, Mom dabbed my head with it, rinsed the blood out, then dabbed again. I can still visualize us there like an illustration in a children's book called "Rinse, Dab, Repeat."

I have sometimes wondered why I was "accident prone" as a child. Could it be that I equated injury with an opportunity for nurturing? If one must be hurt to be held could it also create a fear of affection because of this mental association? I've always had difficulty with displaying or receiving affection.

My mother's aversion to me could have had something to do with the fact that she found out she was pregnant for me at her six-week checkup following the birth of my sister. MY "original sin" was bad timing. She often said I looked like a "skinned rabbit" when I was born. To this day my sister jokingly calls me the "afterbirth" and I retort that Mom saved the best until last. Each year we celebrate a few weeks of being "twins."

I was the first son in the family, but of course it took a while to figure that out. Despite being inundated with females, I must have looked around and saw people, much more like me than different, so I wanted to be a part of this group and I was welcomed at first.

After a few years I started getting the feeling that I was the "odd (little) man out." The girls seemed to want to play together sometimes and I wasn't invited. Even earlier, I recall bathing with my sister who was only ten months older and then suddenly that was not allowed. No explanation was given.

I remember that around age four I was sitting with the same sister on a fence rail and we saw a polar bear running toward us. Terrified, we ran into the house. Of course, there was no polar bear, (not in Michigan) so it was a dream. Yet, it is still as vivid as a real memory - just like my dream of flying around the kitchen with her watching me approvingly. I have my guesses about the meaning of these pseudo-memories, but I leave it to the reader to form their own theories.

At about four or five I started developing different interests from my sisters, but sometimes I still wanted to be included in their activities. On one occasion, a little older and feeling rejected, I defaced two of my sisters' newly-acquired First Communion certificates, (marking the Catholic sacrament). With the indignation of someone deprived of basic social justice, I wrote, "THE GOON" on them.

I obviously didn't take rejection well, but just including me was not enough. At an early age I developed the idea that only an adoring girl could cure my loneliness and emptiness. I was thing-one chasing thing-two. It was a game of tag, and I was "it."

When I reached puberty my definition of adoration started to become sexualized and the search for the ideal female specimen who would not only look perfect, but would always be attentive, began in earnest. By then I also started to realize the benefits of being a boy. I was not expected to help around the house as much as the girls and I took full advantage. My playing baseball (Mom's fervent sports interest) cemented my privileged status. I had finally won her over, one base hit at a time.

Peeping Tom

As a pre-teen, when I wasn't defiling sacred documents and daydreaming about girls, I was mostly playing baseball and other sports. By then I had five sisters, the oldest one in her late teens. All my sisters developed early so I was always surrounded by girls with obvious manifestations of puberty. Of course, this fed my budding interest in female anatomy. I needed a baseline though, something to which I could compare my dream girl. At one point my devotion to research compelled me to do some peeking on my oldest sister. Opportunity presented itself in the form of an antique bathroom door with a keyhole large enough to see through.

One evening I was allowed to nap in my parents' room next to that bathroom because I had a touch of the flu. I crawled out of bed and tip-toed to the bathroom door while she was bathing. I peered through the forbidden portal and was able to see my sister's figure and looked up and down, trying to inventory the parts and reassemble them in a way that added to my understanding of the essence of a woman. Before the gestalt was completed I heard a sound and quickly ran back to bed and resumed my sickly pose.

A few days later another opportunity arose, and I went to the bathroom door to resume my study of the intricacies of the female form. I kneeled to get the best angle only to find that some paper tissue had been crammed into the keyhole. I WAS SO BUSTED!

I ran to my room upstairs taking three steps at a time and sat there waiting for the hammer to come down. I flipped back and forth between thoughts of confessing and expressing remorse, or outright denying any guilt and condemning them for even thinking I would do such a thing. I waited and trembled, waited and trembled. Nothing happened, and two hours passed. Then, two days, and then two weeks.

No one ever said a word. The tissue screamed loudly enough.

Thankfully, my peeping career ended there. Imagine since my name is Tom, me having a reputation for peeping. I would not only be labeled a pervert, but a walking cliché as well. I cringe at the thought of being either.

My interest in eyeing the forbidden did not wane merely because I got caught. Soft pornographic magazines were available at my cousin's house and one of my neighbors about my age commandeered an occasional magazine. Since this was pre-internet we had to find special places to view them and took turns as the lookout in case parents popped in. We were learning the art of deception or maybe just discretion, depending on how one looks at it. We certainly would have been mortified if we had been discovered.

How we react to children and teens regarding their curiosity about the human body is a discretionary matter, but hopefully shaming is not the main or only response. Following are some varying responses.

These Kids Today

Recently, a member of a family I know, a fifteen-year-old boy, was caught by his parents viewing explicit porn on the internet. They discussed it with him calmly and reasonably, even though they felt a little hurt because they had trusted him to only go to approved sites.

He responded by saying that he needed the images to "do his thing." It was obvious he meant masturbation which they had previously told him was perfectly natural and OK. They told him that they didn't approve of pornography and encouraged him to use his imagination instead of images on the internet. He exclaimed, "That would only work if I had total visual recall!"

"That would be a wonderful thing to develop," his dad replied.

The Cold Facts About Skinny Dipping

A group of teenagers I knew through one of my sons went swimming at an old abandoned quarry that was popular for late night skinny dips.

They got mostly undressed when a police officer arrived and busted them for being out after curfew. The officer was professional and very conscientious about his duty. As the cop's headlights shone on the nervous teens, he started giving a long lecture about the importance of obeying the law, especially the curfew, for safety reasons and how it could lead to a life of crime, etc., etc.

He never mentioned the evils of skinny dipping, or implied that this too was a gateway crime. If fact, he acted oblivious to the fact that he was addressing a group of half-naked teenagers. After several minutes one of the boys, who was still in his underwear and shivering in the cool night air, interrupted the cop and asked permission to get dressed. The cop waited until they all got dressed and resumed his lecture without missing a beat.

He called the parents and asked them to come and get their kids. He told the moms and dads how he could "barely keep a straight face" when he was talking to the kids, but he had to "put a little fear in them.". "Protect and Serve Without Shaming" is not a bad motto for a cop.

Budding Artist

As a younger teen I once did a pencil drawing of a nude woman. I was very proud of my artistic achievement, etched in exquisite detail, and I enjoyed the erotic power of creating my own nude companion. I carried her in my wallet to keep her close, sort of like an imaginary friend with limited benefits. We had the perfect relationship for me at that time since I was afraid of real live girls. She couldn't reveal our secret, and neither would I, even under the threat of torture. One day my mother went through my wallet (I'm not sure why) and she found my artwork and ripped it to shreds. It terrified her that I was interested in women this way.

Mom had been sexually assaulted at age thirteen, which I didn't know at the time, but that allowed me to understand her later in my adulthood. When I reached puberty, she was afraid if I appeared to be overtly sexual, but she was also afraid that I might be gay when I wasn't conspicuously in pursuit of girls. Like most mid-teen boys, I would spend a lot of time with buddies, and if we looked like we were having too much fun or showing any affection, she would accuse us of acting silly or gay. Later when I started dating I did not bring girls to the house because, by then, Mom was drinking heavily and was likely to make a scene. The fact that I was seeing girls without her knowledge added to her fears that I was "different."

When she reacted so harshly to my wallet masterpiece it affected me greatly. After that, although I didn't give up my fascination with female nudity, I gave up art altogether.

Innocence Reclaimed

In my psychotherapy practice I was sometimes torn between going deep into my clients psyche and history, or a quick fix in the form of a recommendation to resolve their current problem. It's like cauterizing a wound versus the much longer process of debriding the wound by carefully packing it with a dressing, removing the dressing, and repacking as needed - until it heals from the inside out. As a therapist in a college counseling center, I didn't always have the time to engage in an extended process, so I would occasionally take a more directive approach.

One of my clients was in her late twenties and about to be married. She was becoming depressed because she had been raped when she was in high school and with her wedding a month away, she was acutely aware of her shattered dream of being a virgin on her wedding night. Because she was graduating and leaving the state in a week, I went for the cure.

Once she informed me that she and her fiancé were sexually active I suggested she have a conversation with him and seek an agreement that they abstain from sex until after the wedding. I argued that virginity is not defined by biology but is more a state of mind. It's also a continuum, not an either or. I told her that virginity, like love, cannot be forcibly taken, it can only be freely given. Further, by following my suggestion, she and her fiancé could be "more virginal" on the wedding night. I really would have preferred to acknowledge her pain and allow her more time to work through the issues, but that wasn't possible.

She eagerly agreed to the plan. Unfortunately, I never saw the result because she left campus soon afterwards. I suspect that it allowed at least some temporary relief for these reasons:

1) It put more control in her hands, offsetting some of the loss of control experienced by rape victims.

2) It was a good test of HIS commitment to her. If he couldn't abide by this agreement, he would not have the patience and compassion to support her through times she was affected by her issues from the past.

3) Even if they did not abstain and mutually agreed to have sex, she would be rebelling against my rule, and she would likely feel some sexual empowerment.

The worst outcome would be if she gave into pressure from him and that triggered her shame and she relived some of the trauma. Just in case, I had suggested that she find a therapist in the community in which she would be residing as soon as she arrived there. I hope she is doing well.

Don't Touch That Thing

A student requested counseling because he had recently cheated on his girlfriend and she was threatening a breakup. He attributed his straying to her being too busy with school and work to meet his needs. He said he could never turn a woman down, nor could he masturbate. He said both attitudes came from a passage in the Bible. He recited the relevant quote as, "It's better to spill your seed into the belly of a whore than waste it on the ground." To him this meant that not only was masturbation sinful, but even using a condom was dubious.

His sexual desires always had to be accommodated by a woman and getting caught cheating, pregnancy, STI's, etc. were necessary risks. When I pointed out (even though I'm not a religious counselor) that that passage does not even appear in the bible, he was anxious. I walked him through the issue by showing him the practice of "spilling seed on the ground" was considered a sin in a very specific context. A little research informed us both that it probably meant that a biblical character would not help the wife of his deceased brother get pregnant, so he was shirking his duty to his brother, according to the custom of the time.

Genesis 38:9 "Onan knew that the offspring would not be his; so, when he went in to his brother's wife, he wasted his seed on the ground in order not to give offspring to his brother."

I didn't tell the student what to do, but we eventually agreed he would be better off if he stopped cheating and became more openminded about his options.

The Shame Shadow

"Be not ashamed of mistakes and thus make them crimes."
Confucius — (551-479 BC)

Some of the stories in this chapter have a common theme. They convey how much sexual shame affects us and how insidious it can be. Generally, shameful feelings or thoughts, if not owned, are acted upon in some way - usually as habits or compulsions. For example, many men and women masturbate with visual images or other props, but only a minority to a degree that interferes with other activities or goals. The ones that lose control are usually plagued with guilt and shame which causes them to feel bad when they succumb and worse when they don't. The flip from shamefulness to shamelessness has no middle. If we are to be bad, we want to at least be damned good at it. On the other hand, if we don't see sex as inherently immoral we can be more likely to control and moderate our activity.

Though some stop at the level of their private affair with themselves, others may cheat on their partners. Some are cheating deliberately because of moral failings, but many of them claim they don't really intend to cheat. They say they unintentionally "fell" for the person. Really, it's sometimes more like "jumping." Other times it's like trying to balance a coin on its edge. They put themselves at risk for falling the minute they find the person attractive and still spend time with them. It's not that men and women can't be attracted to each other and be friends, it's a question of what it takes to be able to do that.

You can't balance a coin if you're shaky and self-deceptive. Just about everyone finds people outside their relationship attractive, but the control threshold is crossed when their individual shame is so deep that they become careless. In effect they delude themselves because of shame and the attraction becomes a compulsion. At that point they take the risk of acting out and getting caught.

Shame draws people past their limits because it's excited by the risk of exposure.

A healthy couple can talk about their attraction to other people. Jealousy depends on shame because it grows from insecurity, the feeling of not being good enough. Violating trust is based on the need to affirm we ARE good enough by being bad enough with someone else.

Not Good Enough nor Bad Enough

A college student told me he was about to lose his significant other because he could not stop his use of internet porn. This situation was especially interesting and challenging because he didn't believe he was doing anything wrong, yet he couldn't tell her he was going to continue, and that "she would just have to accept it." Instead, he agreed to stop it, but continued and attempted to conceal it. This strategy failed because he couldn't maintain sufficient control, he got careless, and because she was a Computer Science major. She could track his every move on the internet, and she did.

It gets even more interesting if we also look at her side of the equation. Her objection to his behavior was not on moral grounds, but rather it was based on her own shame. She said it hurt her because it "meant that she wasn't enough for him." Shame has to do with falling short of an ideal – like a shadow that follows us everywhere. It's the only shadow that can overtake light because it is cast by the tremendous power of erroneous beliefs.

In his case he didn't believe the porn was wrong or bad enough to quit, but he didn't feel good enough to assert himself and ask her to accept him as he was. She, on the other hand, interpreted his penchant for pornography as a direct threat to her self-esteem and sense of worth. She erroneously believed that somehow his interest in other women as sex objects was connected to her inadequacies and her imperfections.

Shame thrives on perfectionism.

The healthy thing to do would be for each one of them to stand their ground and test the viability of the relationship. They couldn't do that if they were bound together in shame. In the light of the innocence beam they are both OK as they are; they are good enough. The shame shadow deepens their insecurities by cloaking their inherent worth.

To be clear, I'm not condoning or condemning his behavior. I'm arguing that honesty is essential in a healthy relationship. It's better not to make promises we can't or don't intend to keep. In the light of mutual self-disclosure, they would see if they can accept each other as they are now, and/or if they had the wherewithal to work through these difficult issues together.

For better or worse, 'til shame do us part.

Casualties

Shame is always destructive to relationships. It separates us from others because we keep secrets, even when it would be better to talk with someone. If we define "intimacy" as knowing another person and allowing them to know us, then shame prevents that kind of connection. Shame is even more sinister when it's so deep that we conceal things from ourselves. When we deny the sexual part of ourselves we are not a whole person. Our sexuality takes on a life of its own, outside of our control.

Remember the masturbating girl in my earlier story. She couldn't tell anyone. If she had touched herself in front of her parents in the past and was told "don't do that" then something was missing - namely, context. It would be better to say, "It's not a good idea to do that in front of other people." I know this person as an adult and she overcame her shame but only after some therapy.

Remember the boy who proudly proclaimed his orgasm to his parents? When the boy made his announcement, the Dad provided some context. He implied that the act itself was OK, but discretion is called for in terms of sharing it. The job of parents is to teach what I call "context sensitivity."

One reason some clergy are prone to acting out is that they have no context in which sex is OK. If sex is a part of all of us, then this is not a workable situation. Denial of one's sexual self, combined with the power and emotional closeness with others that a ministry provides, set the stage for acting out. The same applies to those who care for children and teacher-student relationships. Many people believe that "perverts" and pedophiles are attracted to those professions to gain access to victims. In most cases I disagree. It's much more complicated than that. Most of them are attracted to those professions because they want to help people, but they have not resolved their own shame issues. The innocence beam shines brightly on the potential for healing, and sometimes healing takes place. Other times, in the shadows of privacy, shame turns healing intentions into deeper wounds.

Shameful Lapses

I recall an incident with a therapy client that reminded me of the healing intentions gone awry. She disclosed some serious mistakes she had made that I identified with, so I felt a strong emotional connection. She also looked like a girl I had a crush on in high school and never quite got over. Strong empathy and the rekindling of an old flame caused me to reveal my attraction to her rather impulsively, even though I "knew better."

I told her in effect that "although I would never get involved with a client, she was beautiful and that it made working with her more of a challenge." My positive intent was to be honest, (also to give the attraction less power) but the effect was to damage the therapeutic relationship. She understandably felt uncomfortable with this and complained to my supervisor. Although my supervisor was understanding, I felt bad and still do because I let the client down. We had done excellent work until that point. It wasn't her beauty that broke down my boundaries because, as a college counselor, I worked with attractive clients every day. It was our similar shame history that made her so alluring. Shame doesn't like being alone all the time.

In thirty years of practice I had only one other lapse of professionalism. A very attractive client was reciting some of her sexual escapades in vivid detail. It was definitely a TMI situation, but I didn't want an interruption to cause her to feel embarrassed, especially since it was the first session. After a while I got physically aroused. She was a very fit athlete and I guess imagining her sexual gymnastics was just too much for me that day. Fortunately, I had a legal pad on my lap, but I couldn't hide my discomfort.

Not surprisingly, she didn't return for the second session. Arousal is involuntary, so I didn't blame myself for that, but because of my uneasiness with her, I didn't follow up to see if her situation had improved. Her condition was not life-threatening, so I chose the safer path for me of just letting it go. I could have referred her to another therapist, but the explanation would have been a little awkward.

I mention these lapses in my ability to stay mentally on my game for two reasons. One is that I want to convey the idea that no matter how determined we are to do our jobs well, we will sometimes be affected by unresolved issues or normal human responses. Therapists slip - as do other people who supervise, teach, etc.

The inability to keep good psychological boundaries with clients is called counter-transference. I never did anything overt with a client, but I had to be vigilant to keep my personal issues from getting in the way of the treatment. I didn't want to be unprofessional, and I certainly didn't want to be like a psychiatrist I worked with who married three women who had been his clients.

Teachers, clergy, etc. also need to pay attention to how they react to the people they are helping. Compassion is the best human quality but when we feel it, we also sense the vulnerability of the other person. We must be mindful not to exploit that. I often had to point out subtle language nuances to the therapists I trained. "May I have a hug?" is very different from "May I give you a hug?" We must always be mindful of who's needs we are trying to meet in any interaction. This is a good message for parents too.

Another reason I feel free to divulge these personal lapses is that I'm retired – I can't get fired for being candid now. I feel a bit vulnerable though, sort of like former president Jimmy Carter when he was inter-viewed by Playboy magazine and famously admitted he sometimes "lusted in his heart." He got a lot of flak for just being human.

Lead Us Not

As a boy, growing up with some religious influence, I often wondered about the phrase in the Lord's Prayer, "Lead us not into temptation, but deliver us from evil." Does this mean that we are asking not to be led into circumstances that will tempt us at all? Or, does the "but" imply that we'd prefer not to be led there, but if for some reason we are - may the conse-quences not be too harmful. (Don't put that scrumptious dessert in front of me, but if you do – please don't let my cholesterol get too high.)

The latter interpretation makes more sense to me because I can't im-agine a world without some temptation, and the world is fraught with possible negative consequences for our choices we would prefer from which to be delivered. This part of the prayer could be summed up as "Dear God, please don't let our screw-ups screw up our lives."

Relating to sex many people, if not most, make bad decisions or give in to compulsions. Large numbers of people are victims of sexual mis-treatment, mostly in relationships, or from acquaintances. When we con-sider that the majority of instances go unreported in our society, we are under responding to a virtual epidemic. Colleges and other places young people congregate are full of temptation and consequences, yet higher ed-ucation has been mostly ineffective at prevention of sexual misconduct. Victims are the walking wounded among them, crying for help that often doesn't come.

Perpetrators experience serious consequences as well. Recently the pendulum of the U.S. Department of Education under Betsy Devos has swung in the direction of assuring "due process" for perpetrators. Many people believe the government has gone too far in that direction since so many go unpunished already. Nonetheless, countless individuals have lost relationships, jobs or status, or faced criminal charges, because of alleged incidents. There are cases of false accusations, but they are rare. Many of the accused are not people we would generally label as deviant or criminals, and they often enjoy considerable success in other areas of life.

Though they should be legally responsible for their behavior, how much they are to blame morally is a complicated question, and guilt is difficult to prove in "A said - B said" situations. Reform is needed to deal with the many variations in sexual misconduct, so there is always at least some consequence, and a great deal more consistency.

The trend for years has been that handling of complaints needs to be victim-driven. I agree in cases where evidence is not clear. In cases where verifiable evidence is available, we should be more process-driven and consider criminal charges despite the victims wishes. To make such a change we would have to improve the justice system to protect victims from further abuse in court proceedings, such as bringing up their past, etc. Still, one could argue that allowing the victim to always decide the course of action could fail to protect the community from the more violent aggressors.

Loss of Control

People are expected to control their sex impulses in society, but compulsion is the natural state for those who depend too much on external controls. Because of extreme moral beliefs, shame can act like a selective barrier that tries to filter out forbidden thoughts, but also inhibits problem-solving capabilities. When these repressed thoughts reach a critical mass, they break through with great power. People who attempt to live up to impossible standards are the most vulnerable to these powerful internal forces. It's better to ask ourselves, "How can I get these needs met without hurting anyone?" than, "How can I make these needs disappear?" Needs don't disappear, though sometimes they hide behind a thick, dark shame shadow, ready to roll over us the minute our guard is down.

How many clergymen or congressmen do we have to catch with their compulsions exposed before we have an epiphany? SHAME IS THE INCUBATOR OF COMPULSION. The money paid out several years ago by the Los Angeles Diocese alone (over six hundred million dollars) could have helped a lot of people - including the priests who committed the offenses, by developing prevention programs for them. Currently the Catholic Church is embroiled in yet another scandal involving 300 priests over a 70-year period, and the coverups go high into the ranks of the church leadership.

Just last week, after an investigation by the Houston Chronicle, a major scandal erupted over sexual abuse among Southern Baptist ministers. More than 380 clergy and volunteers have been charged with sexual misconduct over two decades, leaving behind more than 700 victims to deal with the aftermath. Other scandals are revealed almost too frequently to keep up with.

How many teachers will have sex with their students before we realize how damaged these perpetrators are, and we should try to help them before they become teachers? How many parents and other caregivers will abuse children before we find a way to curb their menacing shame?

If, indeed, the world is a place full of temptation, we either need to reduce the temptation, or minimize the consequences, or both. Efforts to stifle temptation with puritanical ideas such as modest clothing or segregating the sexes seem ineffective generally, although they might work in some closed communities.

My physician once told me he appreciated growing up in a strongly religious community and he has remained in it his whole life. He beamed when he shared that he didn't kiss his wife until their fifth date. He chuckled as he told me, "When I kissed her she was relieved." Up until then she told him that she thought, "Something must be wrong with him."

For those who don't have or need external structures to support moral behavioral, internal controls must be highly developed. To foster a higher level of moral development in those individuals, we should encourage mature and critical thinking. For these independent thinkers, sexual morality, like all forms of morality, should weigh intentions and consequences heavily to guide their actions.

Even though I'm supporting a relativistic and nuanced moral code, I still believe we are personally responsible for the direct consequences of our deeds. We are obliged to make amends, even if the harmful act was unintentional. In some cases, this could make us criminally accountable, in other cases at least civilly or morally liable. This carries with it an obligation for us to accept justice, compensate, apologize, make amends, etc.

All sexual misbehavior should carry consequences, yet, we would not punish a person who accidentally ran someone over with their car to the same degree as someone who did so deliberately. Consequences would follow, but not based on the same level of criminality. Similarly, we should not judge others' behavior without knowing the context. The renowned feminist, Germaine Greer got in hot water recently for suggesting that sexual assault punishments be reduced. I think she went a bit too far, but she has a point. Some punishment is better than no punishment at all.

Julian Assange, the famous leaker, (Wikileaks founder) allegedly committed two sexual crimes. In one, he started intercourse when his partner was unable to give consent, and in the other he continued after his condom "broke" (I'm tempted to say "leaked") without telling the woman. The charges were subsequently dropped (because he was not available for indictment), although new charges could still be brought if he ever returns to Sweden. Upon hearing this, I thought, "Another highly publicized case is unsettled and the impression that men can get away with it is now even stronger."

Slow Reflections

A man told me that he and a woman were on a date. After dinner she invited him to her apartment and they drank heavily. They crawled into bed together and he started foreplay and she didn't object. He continued to insertion and she still didn't say anything. He finished and went to sleep. When they awoke the next morning, she discovered that they had sex. She was not aware of it when it happened because she was in a black out. She said to him, "You shouldn't do that!"

He left and didn't think that much of it until twenty years later.

He told me it wasn't until the MeToo movement publicized examples of rape that he realized that he had committed a sexual assault. He had been rationalizing all these years that he was just doing what most men would do with a sexual opportunity. He said, "I didn't force her, and I didn't hurt her physically and, in fact, I was trying to give both of us pleasure."

He was blinded at the time by his need to do what he thought was normal for a man. He had learned that if a man turned down an opportunity, he wasn't a real man. At that stage of his life it would have been more shameful not to do it than to go ahead. Like many of his contemporaries, no one had ever taught him how to verbally seek consent. It was all implied. He had unprotected sex and he didn't even consider the following obvious concerns:

1) She could believe that they would sleep together and not have sex.

2) Due to alcohol she could be incapable of deciding.

3) She could not be on birth control.

4) She could have an STI and not be able to warn him.

5) A pregnancy could mean a child out of wedlock or a painful decision to terminate the pregnancy.

Assuming this man is reasonably intelligent, how could he ignore all those possibilities? Certainly, being drunk is a factor but not the most important one. Mostly, he was following a script that he had been taught and he had rehearsed mentally many times. "I meet a girl, I get her alone, we make love, we are both happy, I am a man." It's a mantra leading to a trance that gets acted out with the aid of alcohol. Assuming also that he is a man with some decency - if he had been sober - the trance might have been broken by him realizing she was too intoxicated, or he would have been more likely to notice signs that she wasn't an active participant. He shared with me his sorrow and how he was haunted by her simple words, "YOU SHOULDN'T DO THAT."

His crime was not fully intentional, but we don't have a category for accidental rape because we infer intentionality in most things that people do. "I didn't really mean to do it" could be used as an excuse for any crime and the justice system would collapse. He was very insensitive at the time of his misdeed, but later his sense of compassion prevailed.

Two – The Compassion School for Wayward Boys

"If you want others to be happy, practice compassion. If you want to be happy, practice compassion." - Dalai Lama

What follows is the story of my education from a one-room schoolhouse for kindergarten through college and beyond. At first the connection to sex and relationships may not jump out at you, but it will soon become clear. The story illustrates how compassion cannot be taught by words but must be transmitted behaviorally. Actions really don't speak louder than words, they don't speak at all. They are like electric currents that run through us and rearrange our molecules. They are life-altering.

One Room – One Code

Because we lived in such a remote rural area, my first school (I started at age four) was in an old building, eleven miles from the nearest town. Three of my siblings and I attended the same school which was literally one classroom, one teacher, and all eight grades. And no, we did not have to walk for miles in the snow to attend school – we had skis, and even busses.

The teacher's surname was Fitzpatrick, but we called her "Miss Fitz." She was at least in her late sixties at the time and she taught well into her eighties from what I heard later. Of course, it would have been impossible for her to teach all these students simultaneously, so necessity forged the educational model, and she did the only two things she could – delegate and inspire. She did them both very well. Every new student got the same message on their first day; that each grade had the responsibility to help teach the grade below it, and above all, we don't hurt anyone or let them get hurt.

There were unspoken and implied rules and privileges too. One day I noticed a boy sneaking out a window to go play in a cow pasture. With the moral absolutism of a four-year-old I felt duty bound to report this transgression to Miss Fitz. I was a bit perplexed when she replied, "I guess he decided he could learn more outside today." That statement became the basis of my absorbing one of her other principles of education, namely - that a teacher should never interfere with a real learning opportunity.

Later in the year, overtaken by my own restless craving for adventure, I exited through the same window of possibilities, only this time it involved pigs and lots of mud. When I returned to the classroom I was confident I wouldn't be confronted about my absence, but my wet, muddy clothes would surely elicit some disapproval. Miss Fitz - never short on surprises - just gave me a hug and said, "I think there are some clothes in the closet that might fit you if you want to change." As I walked away I turned back and noticed I had left a sizable mud stain on her dress. I felt a little ashamed and wondered what she would say.

She said nothing. She wore her stains like a badge of honor.

School Spirit

By the time I was ready for first grade we had moved to a suburban area of a midsized city. The transition to a grade-based school was smooth for the first two years. We sat at round tables in groups and had ample opportunity to move around the classroom. Plus, there was playtime!

When I entered the third grade the structure was painfully different. We were shackled to individual desks and the teacher spoon fed us information whether we were able to swallow it or not. One day I just couldn't tolerate it, so I took the eraser on my pencil and pressed on a tooth repeatedly until my gums started bleeding. I was allowed to go to the bathroom to rinse my mouth and I stayed there as long as I could. I vividly recall looking in the mirror, seeing the sacrificial blood, and feeling proud of myself for being so clever in finding a way to escape the torture of Ms. Chase. Like the proverbial coyote caught in a trap, I would have chewed my own leg off to be free.

Fourth grade was even worse! The desks were still there, and the teaching was even more one-directional and regimented. The pace of in-struction was furious, and I noticed that some other students were falling behind, and I could see the intense frustration on their faces.

One day a student asked a question and the teacher answered it, but it was clear to me that the student was still confused. I got up from my desk to demonstrate how to do the math problem and the teacher quickly swooped down the aisle and grabbed me by the arm and took me outside. She shook me violently and said, "You will never do that again!" I was terrified but much worse than that, I learned a lesson that day that no one should ever have to learn from a teacher. Her violence ran through me like high voltage and it lit up an area in my brain that had been dormant. For the first time I knew it was possible to feel hate.

Fifth through eighth grades were relatively uneventful if you don't count emerging puberty and all that goes with it. My classroom landscape of the period was sprinkled with moments of occasional inspired instruc-tion sandwiched between episodes of paralyzing boredom. For multiple reasons my education up to and through then had not prepared me for the large high school in an adjacent city that was the only public high school available. You know the story - small fish getting swallowed up by bigger fish in the deep dark waters of teenage drama and cruelty.

My parents decided I would be better off in the small Catholic school just a few blocks from our house. I transferred there in my sophomore year. Things improved socially, and I could compete in sports in that "Class D" school. Nonetheless, my problem of boredom persisted and a couple of unspeakable tragedies that year sucker punched my whole school into profound numbness. President Kennedy was assassinated and six of our faculty were killed in a head on collision, within weeks of each other.

We had lost our hero and whatever sense of security we had left in a short span of time. So, when I wasn't skipping school I would keep myself amused by debating with the teachers. Some took this better than others. My geometry teacher would praise me, especially when I could complete problems that even he couldn't master. Another faculty, a priest, didn't appreciate me debating theology with him and he suspended me for three days for arguing with him in class.

After that I decided to keep quiet and stay off the radar enough to stay out of trouble. I managed to keep the expectations of the faculty low. They didn't know of what I was capable, and I was more subdued, so they left me alone. I had a good thing going; I could come and go as I pleased.

Occasionally I would make the mistake of bringing attention to myself, but not very often. For example, in one class I accidently got inspired by the challenge of writing a short story with the requirement of submitting it the very next day. I turned in my story only to be accused of plagiarism because no one with my low grades "could have possibly written it."

I made one other mistake in high school, allowing a friend to convince me to take the SAT in my senior year even though college was not solidly in my plans. When the scores arrived, I got a surprise visit from the Principal who came to the class where I was, literally pulled me up out of my desk by my ear and marched me to her office. I had gotten the highest verbal score and the second highest math score in the class. When she ordered me to sit in the chair across from her desk I thought to myself, "I would have probably gotten the highest math score too if I hadn't drunk so much beer the night before."

She proceeded to give me the classic lecture about how much "potential" I had and what a waste etc., etc., ad nauseam. My rather rude response was, "So I might be worth something one day but I'm not worth much right now?" To this day I'm relieved this nun didn't fly over the desk and strangle me. She left an impression, though, because of the anger she expressed. It was almost as highly charged as my fourth-grade teacher's tirade, but this was different. I could tell she cared about me.

With my cavalier attitude about schoolwork, and a penchant for partying, my high school career was a wash. I graduated with a D average and virtually no study habits. The year I graduated the Viet Nam war was in full swing and the draft was on. I enrolled in a community college, but even the fear of mortal combat wasn't enough to override my complacency. I dropped out because I was failing anyway and decided to surrender my student deferment. Within days I was drafted. I blew through two years of military service, fortunately never saw combat first hand, and ultimately came out of it with the wind of the G.I. Bill at my back.

I started college again, if for no other reason than to collect the money. All I had to do was maintain a C average and that's exactly what I did. I had a job at the time that reimbursed me for tuition, so I was making a profit from this venture by double-dipping.

Somewhere in my third year I made another mistake - a big one! I had hung around long enough to contract the disease I call "scholaria." I had always been intellectually curious but had never been academically inspired. By that I don't mean things like just getting the work done on time or jumping through hoops like a trained porpoise; I mean focused intellectual effort driven by a deep sense of purpose. Ultimately the bargain I struck with myself was that I could keep going as long as I believed that my efforts would have a real effect on the world.

Newly endowed with this passion, I started to think about grad school. My earlier undergrad grades made it difficult to get accepted in a top-tier institution but that didn't stop me. By the time my circumstances allowed me to apply a few years later I had decided on the social work/counseling field. Since I lived in Ann Arbor near one of the highest ranked Social Work schools in the nation, I applied there.

I was flatly rejected!

I was determined enough to reapply the following year with better references and a cover letter that grabbed their attention. In it I stated, "I hope you will accept me this time because I'm going to keep applying until you do." Apparently, that display of hubris got me the interview and the rest was easy.

My grad school tenure was marked by academic and practical experiences of the highest quality. Just as important; it forced me to learn how to use computer technology, something not easy for everyone in my generation. Once I saw what computers could do, I was certain they would transform the world and I had to get in stride or become irrelevant. Ever since then my unabashed love for technology has extended my career and my reach.

After grad school I entered the human services arena and stayed in it my entire career until I was able to take early retirement. Continuing a long and enjoyable mission of helping others, I founded and run a non-profit organization that serves youth and helps them – you guessed it – "reach their full potential."

Just like my best teachers and mentors we don't shame them or scare them, we simply tell them the truth and love them while trying to get them to hang around long enough for something to happen. Given my lifelong journey as a student, counselor, and university faculty I have distilled my experience into a few principles that I believe should inform our practice as teachers at all levels of education. With proper credit given to Miss Fitz and others, I submit the following prescriptions of pedagogy:

1) <u>Students should be given more responsibility for their learning.</u> One way I promote this is by giving my college students "jobs" at the beginning of each semester. They have titles like "local news hound", the student who reports on local events that are relevant to the subject, or even "the class clown" who must come to class each week with jokes. I tell the clown that the jokes better be relevant, but if not, then they must be exceptionally funny. Then there is the "political reporter" who is charged with reviewing public policy initiatives to determine how youth will be affected.

2) <u>No one gets hurt.</u> This means physically of course, but also emotionally. Our rules of engagement in my classes include a requirement to honor the intelligence of others. Since we arrive at conclusions based on

what we've learned thus far, bad ideas are just good ideas under development.

3) Everyone learns from everyone. As teachers we are only one source of information. With the proliferation of the internet we're probably not even the most up-to-date source available. So - get humble.

4) Students have no obligation to learn or get high grades. We can complain all we want about students not caring but they have the right to get what they want out of college. If they want to barely pass to get the degree to enter a field of their choice, that's fine. If they are in school just to keep parents off their backs, that's a good reason too. If we're doing our job, scholarship will be contagious.

5) Embrace technology. It can be today's window to the irresistible cow pasture for some students, but it's not going away. Our role is not to stop it, but to keep fighting to assure it's used for good purposes.

The idea that all we ever need to know we learned in kindergarten has long been an American truism thanks to the popular 1980's book by Robert Fulghum. We might expand Fulghum's dictum just a little by saying, "All we ever need to know we learned in the one-room schoolhouse we call 'our world.'" The academic part of that world should be collaborative, rich, diverse, and sometimes muddy; which is to say that in one way or another, we should all be Miss Fitz.

What did I learn from my educational journey? Mainly two lessons, one good and one bad. Both are general life lessons, but also relate to sex and relationships. First, I learned that helping others and compassion is demanded of all of us – even boys. Years of regimented, regressive educational experiences and negative messages about competition and masculinity could not uproot the lesson planted by Miss Fitz - helping others is not an exception, it's the rule.

Second, I learned that boys are often given more leeway than girls. Even Miss Fitz bought into the idea that "boys will be boys." This manifested itself in my being allowed to do what I wanted if I didn't cause trouble. Through all my primary and secondary education this was obvious, and I took full advantage of it. Of course, later I had to struggle to overcome some bad habits but eventually managed to do so. It seems unfair that girls must <u>be good,</u> but boys often get rewarded for just <u>not being bad.</u>

Three - Lovesick

"Don't cry because it's over, smile because it happened." - Dr. Seuss

My first real crush was in the sixth grade. Her name was Cathy and she was amazingly cute. She had a pixie haircut and the prettiest big eyes, and she wore socks that went up to her knees. One day she had black socks on with panda bear faces on the knees. She looked like an anime character come to life. I was in love! My secret Saturday morning cartoon wish had come true!

She lived about ten blocks down the street from us. I knew where her neighborhood was because I saw her get off the school bus every day. In fact, one reason I liked her was the way she looked when she jumped off the bottom step of the bus and skipped down the street. She always seemed so happy. I vowed that I, Tom Terrific the sixth-grade superhero, would make her even happier.

One afternoon I put on my best shirt – navy blue, long sleeves, button-down collar, and I tucked it into my jeans. They were the only jeans I had that didn't have holes. I checked them all over. No food stains or grass stains. I was good to go.

I walked to her house rehearsing different lines…if someone besides her answered the door.

"Is Cathy home?" Pretty lame.

"May I come in and talk to Cathy?" Even lamer.

"Can Cathy come out and play?" You gotta be kidding! I'm a sixth grader not a kindergartener!

"Get out of the way damn it, I want to see your daughter, now!" I don't think so.

And if Cathy answers the door, I'd say something really cool like, "Hi Cathy, I go to school with you."

I arrived and knocked on the door. A man answered. No Cathy there. Oops – Wrong house.

I got my nerve up again and went to the next house. It was a big place with double doors and a brass door knocker. I tried the knocker and waited, but no answer. I pushed the doorbell button and a woman opened the door.

She said, "May I help you?"

I said, "Do you know a Cathy? She said yes, I'll get her. She let me in and smiled, and she didn't seem to mind that I was there at all. She said, "Cathy is upstairs" I'll call her….

"Cathy - a nice little boy is here to see you."

I'm thinking, 'A NICE LITTLE boy'- Lady, I happen to be eleven years old!!! And NICE? Ha!" She obviously didn't know about my plan to give her daughter a big ol' smooch on the cheek.

So, I was in the foyer, leaning against the wall, waiting for Cathy and in a minute or so she came bouncing down the stairs with a cool pair of dinosaur socks I never saw before. (Now that was awesome - a girl with dinosaur socks!)

When she got right up to me, I stood up straight as a stick. I was about to say something about the T-Rexes on her socks, but she looked at me and said, "Oooooh!" She was looking at my arm, so I looked at it and saw a big streak of white paint on my sleeve. They had just painted the wall and it was still wet!

I don't know what we talked about for the few seconds after that because I was backing out the door the whole time. I ran all the way home hoping no one would see me full of paint. I got home and tossed the shirt in a trashcan, a fitting place for a memory-stained garment.

I was talking with a twelve-year old just the other day and I asked him what he thought the hardest part of growing up as a boy is and he said, "Talking to girls. I get so nervous I can't think straight."

I told him, "Yeah, I totally get it, but it gets better." I didn't tell him that it took me decades.

The Love Dance
My middle school was typical in its social activities including the school dances. Oh, the dances! I remember the decorating committees. Ours' was always chaired by Susie Parker. She volunteered for everything because by 7th grade she was already a woman who knew what she wanted. She took charge. She ran the school, even the teachers.

We had an under-the-sea theme for one of our dances and there were fish and other sea creatures and seaweed hanging from the steel beams all over the gym. The old gym kinda' smelled like sea weed and sweaty gym clothes. Actually … sea weed and sweaty clothes after an oil spill.

You couldn't reach the hanging sea creatures so one guy, Jimmy, got a coat hanger and a broom from the locker room and made a fishing pole. He caught one before a teacher tackled him. I couldn't figure out if that thing he caught was supposed to be a shark or a catfish, but we never saw Jimmy again after that night. We thought maybe he was buried in a trunk with chains around it at the bottom of the sea, or the teacher made him walk the plank or something.

JUST KIDDING ABOUT THAT LAST PART. He was back in school Monday morning.

Jimmy was the guy in our class who NEVER followed the rules and got away with it. He was always making fun of the girls looks and saying gross things, but they seemed to like him anyway.

We had "Sloppy Joe" day in the cafeteria every Thursday. They were greasy but so good! When the bell rang we would race to the cafeteria almost knocking each other down to get in line first. Jimmy knew which girls to ask to help him get around the "two sloppy joe rule." He would go up and down the line and whisper to the some of the girls to get two, even if they only wanted one. He would end up with five or six extra Sloppy Joes and if he couldn't eat all of them he would sell some. I got on his good side and got them for free sometimes, but he would wave it in front of my face and make me say please – like HE would ever say please. Maybe you knew someone at your school who seemed to get away with stuff like that?

I could fill the whole night with Jimmy stories but back to the dance....

Ok, so meanwhile predictably for those days, boys were on one side of the gym and the girls on the other.

Everyone is wondering "who's gonna' be first" to take that long lonely walk across the room with everyone watching. You wonder about all the little things that could go wrong. You know, things like, "Will my tongue freeze up and I won't be able to speak? Or...are my pants gonna' fall down?" You know – little things like that.

I went first once, at a dance earlier in the year. I walked over barely able to put one foot in front of the other and asked Jenny Gardner, one of the popular girls. I picked her because she was one of the girls who wasn't taller than me and because she was looking up and around like she wanted someone to ask.

"Would you like to dance?" I said. Ugh. (How original).

She said "no," but I was prepared for that contingency. I had my answer ready. I said, loud enough for others to hear, "I wasn't really asking YOU to dance, I just wanted to know if you LIKE to dance."

Of course, it didn't help me save face with everyone else, and it didn't make the walk back to the safe zone any less embarrassing - but I felt less of a sting by not giving Jenny the full satisfaction of shooting me down in front of everyone.

I never thought much about it but what if you're one of the people waiting to be asked? You might be wondering…

"Will it be me? What should I do if I like them?

What if I don't like them, or I'm not sure if I like them?

And do I really want to be the first one out there?"

It's funny how when we're scared we don't think about the other person being scared.

Love at First Bite

Babysitters can be amazing when you're thirteen and they're not much older than you. One summer we vacationed at a lake and our parents went out in the neighboring town and left us with a sixteen-year-old sitter. I was instantly taken with her and impulsively found ways to make it known. We all went swimming and I broke my personal record for holding my breath as I swam under the surface to her and gently bit her butt. She laughed which only emboldened me and helped me believe I could find a way to win her heart.

Later in the cottage kitchen, I accidently dropped a bottle of ketchup and she heard the crash of the breaking glass. Me being a little opportunist; before she could get to the room I spread ketchup on my arm to make it look like blood. Only she could provide the kind of first aid I needed at the time and it didn't require medical skills. When she realized my ruse, she laughed again and gave me a hug. The rest of the evening is a blur, but I bet it involved other antics to gain her attention, and it may have been the dawn of my pubescent romantic awakening.

First Love or First Place

A few, mostly unrequited crushes in middle school and high school almost killed my confidence but giving up was out of the question. In my sophomore year I saw the epitome of womanhood and any consideration of quitting was erased. I instantly knew I could never be happy unless she was mine.

I had seen her once before when I was younger and at a different school. She was in a movie theatre sitting with one of my buddies. I wondered at the time how he could be with her. I was better looking, and I didn't even know he knew any girls, let alone was dating.

I continued to admire her from a distance until one day I accidently did an experiment in geometry class. She sat right in front of me that day but there was quite a bit of space between our desks. I slouched down in my seat as I often did. I noticed that my knees were almost touching her butt. Like planning a space mission, I was using good geometric calculations to determine how much more slouching it would take for me to land my knees carefully on her butt cheeks. I had to squirm so low in my seat I could imagine my grandmother saying, "Quit slouching, you're going to ruin your posture!"

I probably would have told my grandmother that I didn't care if I was the Hunchback of Notre Dame for the rest of my life if this experiment succeeds.

It did kind of succeed....

"We have Contact."

"Perfect landing."

Now - wait for reaction.

Ten-second check – "No response."

30 second check – "She shifted a little but still making contact."

One-minute check – "Houston, we have a problem!"

She sat up abruptly, separating herself from my knees. Her hand shot up!

"Mayday! Mayday!"

I bolted upright to a position even my Gramma would approve of; hoping to the heavens that she would think my interplanetary contact was totally accidental. Still in experimental mode, I quickly thought of all possible hypotheses:

"Maybe she didn't notice – not likely."

"Maybe she was ok with it – then why did she pull away AND RAISE HER HAND?"

"Maybe she was OK with it - BUT there's a time limit that no one ever told me about?"

"Maybe she thinks I'm a pervert – but wouldn't she have at least given me a dirty LOOK?"

I imagined her saying, "Mr. Workman - Tom put his knees on my butt…. and he is RUINING HIS POSTURE!"

None of those things happened. She asked him a question about geometry.

Later, my notes from the experiment read:

"Mission required extensive physical effort and risk of permanent disfigurement. Destination may involve danger. Planet has soft warm surface. May be habitable. Results inconclusive. Object requires further exploration."

We had been "intimate" for a moment (so I thought), but she still seemed light years away. One Saturday in my Junior year. I somehow mustered the courage to ask her on a date. To my delight, she agreed!

She had dated lots of boys by then and I was certain she had much more sexual experience than me. We went to a movie and afterwards I drove us to a popular "parking" spot. A few minutes of conversation was enough, I thought, then I could make my well-rehearsed move. After some idle chat I leaned over and pulled her close. I aimed my lips at hers and set them on course for docking. She pulled away, startled, and said, "What are you doing!?"

Because I expected a totally different response I did what many people do when caught off guard – I told the truth. "I d-don't know". I stammered. It turned out she had no more experience than me and neither of us had the ability to discuss this beforehand and set expectations or boundaries. After several long minutes of awkwardness, I drove her home and we didn't speak until I dropped her off in front of her house. We said, "Good night" almost simultaneously. We were lying.

We crossed paths several times over the years after that, but we could never synchronize our lips or our lives. She showed interest at one point when she was divorced, but I was married. She told me that as long as I was married, we couldn't see each other. My fantasies about her lasted through all my single years and my married years, until she died of cancer 20 years later. "Until death do us part" is not just a vow of intentions in wedlock; sometimes, it's the epitaph of an unfulfilled dream.

Bluster and Bravado

As an older teen I became very competitive and more confident. One time I was with two male friends at a popular girl's house and it was class picture time. She offered each of us a picture and we took them. My buddies stuck it in their wallets, but I hesitated and said, "I'd like you to sign it." She didn't want to, so I insisted, "If you won't sign it. then I don't want it." She not only signed it, but wrote, "I love you!" on it. I owned my buddies for the rest of the week.

Not long after the above-mentioned photo-op the County Beauty Pageant took place. I attended the ceremony only because I had dated two of the girls who were contestants. When they tied for first-runner-up I beamed with egotistical pride. The feeling of elation didn't last long. When I approached them to congratulate them, the newly-crowned queen was standing behind them with her congratulatory entourage. I looked at her and immediately thought, "Why am I not good enough to date the winner?" The buzz was killed, but the powerful need for female attention and admiration was given new life. I would just have to aim a little higher.

My streak continued after that. I had some girlfriends and more freedom to spend time alone with them. I had forgotten about the 4-F's and milestones. Those nagging drumbeats went dormant for a while. I felt less pressure to prove myself. One time when my parents were out of town for the weekend, I had a few friends over including my girlfriend and we listened to music and hung out. Later that night I laid down on our big overstuffed sofa with her and we held each other. We sank deep into the cushions. It was warm and nice. It felt like standing near a fireplace on a cold day, but better. Who needs a fire? She glowed, and she was warm.

The music in the background was a Beatles song, called "And I Love Her." I heard the lines in the song:

"A love like ours could never die. As long as I have you near me."

I was so content and happy just to be holding her that I didn't even think about going any further. I didn't know it at the moment, but the song should have been more like Agnus Carlsson's "One Last Time" which I heard on YouTube recently. In the song she laments...

"Please just let me hold you.

Let me hold you, one last time."

But the love DID die despite what the Beatles said – and the "one last time" that Agnus would have tried to warn me about came sooner than I expected.

A few days later I was walking down the hall at school feeling good and flipping the locks on the lockers as I went by. I looked up and there she was kissing a guy.... Of all people - Joey! He wasn't a good guy because I had heard him talk disrespectfully about girls before. In fact, he was a jerk. Seeing them together with their arms wrapped around each other, looking at me like kids caught sneaking candy would have been funny, but it hurt too much. I sure wished they hadn't seen me, but it was too late.

After a few months my innocence beam dimmed and none of those status dates or the sweet sofa liaison counted anyway, because unlike some of my schoolmates, I was still a virgin. I felt like a coward by then, but later as a mature adult, I would come to realize that I was just afraid of something that should instill fear. After all, sex can bring life and sometimes death.

Backrubs and Boobs

Although I had dated all those pretty, popular girls, I had virtually no sexual experience. I hadn't even reached second base and it felt like the bottom of the ninth inning with the bases loaded and two outs. Down three runs, it was my turn at bat. It was all on me and I didn't want to let the team down, and I certainly didn't want to disappoint my imaginary fans.

With this kind of pressure, I pursued girls with even more zeal. By the summer between my Junior and Senior year of High School I was on a mission. One evening I met a girl at a party and she was out of high school and had her own apartment. She gave me the address and I visited her there the next night. We laid on her couch and starting kissing with amateurish passion. I didn't know the right angle to tilt my head or how to navigate the noses, but apparently it was enough for her to become aroused. Coming up for air, she said, "I will do anything for you."

I checked the menu in my head and they were all dishes I hadn't tried, so like a fussy eater, I went with the safe choice. "I'd like to give each other back rubs," I said. That was a good selection because it meant I didn't have to face her. Affection du jour, with a little embarrassment a la carte. Maybe she wouldn't sense my embarrassment through her fingers or mine. I few days later I called her, but she made some excuse for not being able to go out with me. I must have rubbed her the wrong way.

Shortly after that experience I met a girl at a roller rink one Friday night. My buddy and I followed her and her girlfriend to a secluded spot and me and my "date" stayed in my car and he went with the other girl to hers. After some preliminary kissing (I was improving) my partner took her t-shirt off. No bra and beautiful, perky breasts. I touched them and squeezed them and although nervous, I thought I was doing OK.

It seemed that it was not enough for her though because she said, "You know, guys usually kiss them, don't you?" I assured her that I knew that, and I was just "taking my time." We never got any further. Her boyfriend (that she never told me about) suddenly showed up with several of his buddies and threatened our lives, so we left. I wanted a sex life even if it killed me. Life and Death.

There were more adventures that summer and my senior year included more episodes of trial and terror, but by the end of that school year, with the help of alcohol as a confidence builder, I made some strides. I had the foreplay thing down pretty well, but still hadn't gone all the way. I started to think, "Maybe my mother was right – maybe I AM different."

Barely Legal Meets Legally Bare

I lived in the Midwest at the time of high school but one of my older sisters had moved to California. The summer after graduation she invited me to spend some time with her in the San Francisco area. I graduated early so I was seventeen. I was still a virgin, but I was determined to change that. I had been close to experiencing intercourse a few times but either I was too afraid, or the girl decided for me. I happened to be in the perfect place to try to have sex for the first time, the Bay Area in the heyday of the sexual revolution!

Although I exuded confidence generally (especially after a few drinks), I sometimes froze when it was time to approach women. But here in this hedonistic paradise even I could probably cross the threshold to real man-hood. Topless bars had just been legalized in my sister's county and I was able to use her car to visit them. I told her I was going to church, and in a way, I was. Sex was my religion at the time and I worshiped women. I was underage but was rarely asked for I.D. since I looked older than most of my peers.

One Sunday night I found a new bar and started drinking and dancing. It was a small crowd, mostly women. A gorgeous blond was occupying the stage and I glanced at her undulating naked form off and on, while I danced and drank with the other women. After a while I ran out of money, so I told the bartender I had to leave. He told me not to worry, that the drinks were "on the house." I hoped it was because he thought I was a "babe magnet" and good for business.

Apparently, the pull WAS strong that night. I had a couple more drinks at the bar and got up to leave. The dancing blonde jumped off the stage, walked up behind me, spun me around (she was still naked from the waist up) and said, "Don't you try to leave here without me! Wait, I'll be done soon."

I thought, "Am I f-ing dreaming? Would my first time be with a god-dess that people pay money just to see?"

After the shock wore off I realized this was really happening, so I got my sophisticated dude pose back on. I waited and a few minutes later we walked out of the bar, our arms locked. Just then, a limousine pulled up to the curb. She abruptly pulled her arm away and said, "Oh shit, that's my sugar daddy. I gotta go!"

Coitus interruptus involuntarium!

I had a few other close calls that summer, but my social life was quarantined when I went into the Army that Fall. Not many dating opportunities in boot camp. Lots of beer though. I could drink at the NCO club with or without money. They had a payroll deduction plan – drink all you want today, and have it automatically taken out of your check at the end of the month.

It wasn't until six months later that I finally broke the losing streak, but I lost much more than my virginity. My innocence and compassion sank along with it and a dark chapter began.

Four - The Terrible Twenties

Believing that I could make my own rules almost led to my destruction as an adult, but the capacity for compassion eventually saved me from myself. There are differing views, even among women, on compassion as it relates to gender:

"I believe that women have a capacity for understanding and compassion which man structurally does not have, does not have it because he cannot have it. He's just incapable of it." - Barbara Jordan

"In my view, the best of humanity is in our exercise of empathy and compassion. It's when we challenge ourselves to walk in the shoes of someone whose pain or plight might seem so different than yours that it's almost incomprehensible." - Sarah McBride

While I had deep compassion for people, I sometimes lacked empathy for women. I was taught that they were too different, and that I could never understand them anyway. Despite my having five sisters, they remained a mystery. Even today the idea persists. A young man recently posted on Facebook:

"Women will never understand the male mind, just like we will never understand the female mind."

Women are stereotyped as both incomprehensible and indispensable. "You can't live with them, and…"

Because of our society's boy/girl apartheid, they were already "the other" by the time I was twelve, and if I was strongly attracted to them physically it was way too easy to objectify them even more. Shame demands that we reduce people to a thing, so we can do things TO them. We do this in war by naming people "the enemy." We do it in the sales field by calling them "prospects." In seeking sex partners, when we see someone as primarily a man or woman, we are already part way to dehumanizing them. In contrast, when we can connect human to human we do things WITH people.

When asked about dating, the famous model, Tyra Banks, once said, "I don't know how to be sexy on a date. Put up a camera and a wind machine, and I'll give you sexy. Put me at a dinner table with some candlelight and the moon shining in and, oh, I will give you dork." Tyra is doing this self-objectification consciously for the purposes of her career, but too many of us do it unconsciously for purposes of trying to feel connected without getting too close. Objectification is intimacy for beginners.

Since fantasy, flirting, and sometimes sexual activity, can be forms of pseudo-intimacy, the sex industry thrives. People use prostitutes and porn to mimic closeness. People don't need props to achieve orgasm, we can do that just fine by ourselves. The appeal of porn and sex workers is that we can pretend that someone else is involved with our shame - an accomplice.

The classic chump in some movies is the guy who visits a prostitute and wants to talk before sex. Sometimes they never get to the sex because the talking is cathartic, or because it breaks the trance that led the customer to the prostitute in the first place. Shame mocks our hunger for intimacy. He paid for sex but only got a conversation. "How pathetic," some might think. I agree with the famous sports writer, Rich Eisen, who says. "Nothing trumps good conversation."

Misery Loves Company

My terrible twenties were profoundly lonely. I was looking for someone to mirror my own shame. Misery loves company, but mine wanted an equal partner. The loneliness of being away from home when I was in the Army was unbearable and made life seem empty. I had the possibility of seeing combat at the time, and death loomed on the horizon. I had to find someone, or I would die alone, a pathetic eunuch.

My time had come to finally prove that the skinned rabbit was lovable, and sex seemed like the only real proof. I was like the virgin-lover looking for evidence on the blanket, except I was looking for tangible evidence of my fuck-ability. I was profoundly isolated.

People who don't know if they are sexually needy or lonely can be dangerous. When I was in the Army I visited a Mexican border town with some other soldiers. We hung out in bars where prostitutes were available. That night I drank up most of my money, so I didn't have much left. When a woman approached me, I negotiated a very low rate with her. We proceeded to her room and I was too drunk to get it on. She was very pissed off because of the double insult. I had diminished her business-woman role AND her sexual role. She screamed something at me in Spanish and then called me a "son of a bitch" in perfect English.

In that episode neither my human side nor my sexual side was satisfied, and neither was hers. It was almost poetic justice when I got back to the base and discovered I had gotten close enough to contract a case of the "crabs." Those little creatures didn't mimic closeness, they unabashedly dug right in.

Not long after that I found the perfect person for me at the time. She was one that I could have sex with because I didn't revere her too much, but also one who needed someone to ground her. She had lost her mother recently and was desperate to have a transitional object. She had joined the military to escape her demons, but they followed her, just like mine did.

It was a fair trade. I would try to make a stable person out of her and she would help heal my shame, or at least learn to override it. We got married and it lasted for several years but it was impossible from the beginning. Neither of us could grow up despite having a child together and good careers. It was a ten-year epic attempt, but the marriage sizzled and sparked and finally blew up.

The remaining years of my stint in the Army were zombielike in my search for meaning and manhood. The years that followed my departure from the service were the same. Despite still being married, and working by day, I moon-lighted as Mr. Hyde. I still chased women and occasionally visited prostitutes, sometimes again, too drunk to perform. This was no longer a quest for the perfect woman, it became a search for the perfect sexual experience, even more detached from partners and my own humanity.

My wife and I slid down a treacherous path. We took on the bumps and bruises of two people looking for something from each other that neither possessed. We started looking elsewhere. We had affairs and fights. We were incredibly cruel to each other. I finally left to save my own life.

I felt like the boy in a movie called "Ordinary People." He was sailing with his brother and a storm came up and capsized their boat. In the opening scene they showed him underwater trying to save his brother, but it became apparent that he would either save himself, or they both would drown. He had survivor's guilt about leaving his brother behind and so did I after the separation. Having to leave my nine-year-old daughter was the most painful thing I have ever experienced. I also had an amazing sense of relief. The chance for a do-over. Two months later I had to renew my driver's license. When I looked at the photo I thought, "Damn, I'm smiling and there's a twinkle in my eye I haven't seen for years."

As I said earlier, my ex wasn't the problem. Escaping the marriage didn't fix me; it only made me more able to make my own mistakes with no one to interfere or blame. I made lots of them. I tried to exploit women one after another, the self even more split. I was making up for lost time and reliving my adolescence. I was going to sleep with as many "girls" as possible, except I wasn't seventeen; I was thirty.

This period reminds me of a stayover at my cousin's house one summer. We were fifteen and we were always competitive. We went to the roller rink and we had a contest about who could skate with the most girls. We tied at thirty-two, but we argued about whether skating with the same girl more than once counted. We never settled that debate. It got even more intense. For a few years, every summer we would try to steal each other's girlfriends. We usually did.

So, at thirty, now single, I was going to be the most prolific lover ever known. In my spare time I was going to also save the world. I was split completely in two - the sinner and the saint vying for awards. A Nobel Prize and an Adult Video News trophy in the same year would top it off. I was able to help people in my job, but nights and days off were just for me. I got greedy, dating more than one woman in a single day and going for more than one at the same time. I did that once, just because I could, but another time it didn't quite work out.

I was in a bar (I was sober by then but still went to bars looking for women) and I sat with two women and we started conversing. Within minutes they told me they belonged to a strict religious group and it was a big deal for them to even be in a place like this. When the topic of sex came up we shared our views. They believed in sex only in marriage, but at least in a committed relationship. I tried to convince them that sex was not immoral if people were kind to one another and they were honest. I even invoked the name of Jesus and said I didn't think he cared about that as much as he wanted people to love and help each other. Is this a real case of "taking the Lord's name in vain" by invoking religion for my own selfish purposes?

It worked, at least with one of them. We went to her apartment in her car and we negotiated a sexual agreement on the way. She was concerned about the physical pain intercourse might cause. She said her husband was "very big" and it often hurt. I told her she didn't have to worry about that with me. It was the one and only time in my life I tried to convince a woman I had a small penis.

I had addressed her concerns and we were heading for the bedroom and there was a knock on her door. It was the other girl, who was worried about her. They sat and visited for what seemed like forever, so I finally said. "Either we go to bed now or I will have to leave. Better yet, what if we all go to bed?"

That didn't go over very well. They told me to leave but at least I was able to negotiate a ride back to pick up my car. We didn't say much during the ride, but I appreciated their basic decency. I had pushed them to their limit, but they didn't leave me stranded. Little things matter when we need saving.

Cowboys and Freud

All those years I never intended to hurt people, quite the opposite. I always felt my purpose was to make the world a better place. I just had theories about my manhood that needed to be tested. By then those messages about ultra-masculinity were sort of in my DNA. Besides peers, this was aided in my teens by my two uncles who were rugged individualists. They were actual cowboys and rodeo performers. They were also notorious womanizers. They were my mother's brothers and she idolized them. Despite her sexual hang-ups, she thought THEY could do no wrong.

These mixed messages about being a real man vs. a good man were incompatible, and I was constantly at war with myself. To be a man I must be "successful" with women, but to be a good man I had to care about others and help them whenever I could.

I had been in pursuit of pleasure as an end in itself; it became my calling. Once we become used to having sex it's easy to start thinking we can't possibly live without it. In a way, we can't. Sex is incredibly pleasurable, and we want to do it much more than it would take to reproduce and keep the species alive. In religious terms, since God has a special relationship with humans, he guaranteed our proliferation by making sex pleasurable. In evolutionary language, humans who enjoyed sex were likely to produce others who enjoyed sex. We multiplied like rabbits – we were naturally selected for coitus.

Perhaps Sigmund Freud had the best explanation. One of his least-discussed ideas was what he called "overdetermination." According to him it meant that everything we do has more than one motivation.

Imagine you are sitting in your office. You are a little bit thirsty but that's not enough for you to get up and walk fifty feet to the water cooler, fill a cup, and drink it and walk all the way back. A little later you start feeling isolated. You could use some social contact, but both of these needs combined still aren't enough to overcome your inertia. A few minutes later you think about the pretty secretary whose desk is only twenty feet past the cooler. She is visually stimulating. Finally, with all three motivations, there's enough potential payoff to get you up and going.

The concept of overdetermination applies to everything. We eat for nutrition but also pleasure. We sleep for rest, but also escape. We do things for multiple reasons even if we don't know what some of them are.

During my sexual safari of my twenties I was emotionally deprived. It didn't help that I was married at the time to a woman who, like my mother, sometimes questioned my worth. The more she put me down, the more I sought other women to build me up. I don't blame either of them for MY actions because they were doing the best they could at the time too. We all had serious issues. Interestingly, my ex was raised around boys and I was raised around girls. How much this factored in I don't know, but our mere presence seemed to trigger profound insecurity in each other. We both were drinking heavily which led to high drama and intense cruelty toward each other.

It also didn't help that my mother repeatedly said that I looked like a you know what when I was born. Periodically, she and my grand-mother would debate if I was turning into a handsome boy or not. They took different sides on different days. I have too - my whole life!

The misogynistic messages I received growing up didn't help either. In the seventh grade I hung out with a group of boys. One of them was taller than the rest, an exceptional athlete, and a good student. He was our leader and we blindly followed. One day we were discussing whether to join the 4-H Club, an organization in our school promoting positive youth development. Our leader said that he would rather join the 4-F club. We took the bait and asked him what that was. He replied with a smirk, "That's what you do with girls. You find 'em, feel 'em, fuck 'em, and forget 'em." The other boys all seemed to laugh.

I wanted to confront him, but peer pressure stifled my gender justice reflex. Besides, I was outnumbered and insecure.

The Hunt

Being aware of all the negative messages I received growing up wasn't enough. Despite my resistance, these messages invaded my personality. Being married wasn't a deterrent either. The search continued, even after the divorce. After that, I was single for the first time in ten years. When I chose to leave, I thought my drinking would get better. I had tried to quit or slow down with her, but we kept playing off each other. "I will if you will," but we both didn't. My drinking got worse and I didn't have her to blame any-more. After a series of scary encounters, I finally quit drinking about a year after the divorce.

Heavy drinking slows down emotional development. I was a seventeen-year-old trapped in the body of a thirty-year-old. This became evident when I got a job as a counselor working with teens. I couldn't avoid the realization that regarding dating, sex, and women, I was in the same place they were. This epiphany, along with a few terrifying experiences scared me into abstinence from booze. I stayed alcohol-free for three months on my own. I was sober but miserable, so I got some help.

One of the most frightening experiences involved an evening of drinking and smoking pot. I was on my way home and was very hungry (it was the strong weed, probably laced with PCP) so I stopped at a restaurant and placed a double order of pasta. Before my food even arrived, I started thinking that I might have raped someone earlier in the evening. I hadn't even been with a woman that evening, but the thoughts persisted. I became paranoid and I started thinking that the police were coming any moment to arrest me. It was so freaky, I got up quickly and left. Walking away from good pasta was bad - but getting a glimpse of this terrible dark side of myself was horrifying!

It was only a few days later that I stopped drinking (weed too) and I haven't since, spanning a period of decades. Now that I was sober, and because I was soon dating women of higher status, whom I had not met in pickup bars, I was certain my sexual adventures would take on a more genteel quality.

Discretion didn't kick in immediately, though. I was in Ann Arbor Michigan at the time and for a heterosexual male in a town with so many open-minded women, it was a virtual field day. Sometimes I was still using women to stroke my ego and prove my manhood. Even sober, the bars beckoned me occasionally. I recall one situation in detail that cured my bar habit and taught me to filter the alluring calls of the night.

Seeing Red

I went to a dance club around ten o'clock one night. It was known as a "meat market." In case some of you don't know, that's a pickup bar.

Honestly, I didn't know if I was more horny or lonely that night- maybe both- but I was ready to roll the dice.

I got there and I'm leaning against the bar (you know that position where you're leaning, and your legs are crossed casually so you look like you're relaxed). "Hey, look at me, I'm just chillin'. I don't need you but if you're real nice I might do you a favor and let you be with me." Yes, that one little position says all that.

So, I'm scoping out the dance floor from this strategic position and I see this stunning woman in a sensual red dress. She's looking Victoria Secret sexy but less forced. She had bright red lipstick on too, and beautiful black hair. The way she moved was almost hypnotizing me. Someone once said that "dancing is like poetry with arms and legs." That's what it felt like, but she had a lot more than just arms and legs in her poem. I couldn't wait for the next stanza.

Her skin was glowing from the dancefloor lights and she was showing just enough of it that my imagination didn't have to strain itself. I thought, "This woman is bliss personified." She could bring that perfect sexual experience I'd always wanted but never quite found.

I went over near where she was and started barely moving my head to the music until I got in sync with her. She pretended she didn't notice me, but I could tell she did – because every time she spun around she made sure her body was in a direct line with me, front or back. "Nice view in this place," I thought. Still no eye-contact though.

I gradually worked my way closer, making myself go as slow as I could. At one point our eyes met and locked on to each other. Within seconds we both knew we were moving together on that dance floor and everybody else was just background. We danced through a couple of fast songs and then a slow song started. I didn't say a word; I just reached out my hand and we met halfway. We sort of melted into each other and I could tell she was really liking it and so was I. It was electric.

Her hair had that freshly washed smell with a tiny hint of vanilla. I wanted to smell it forever. Her skin had the nameless sweet odor I can only call female extract. It was like when you're eating great ice cream and you know you've had enough, but you keep going back for more because you don't want the taste to stop.

After a minute or so I barely brushed her cheek with a kiss, then timing it just right - the neck. Before the song was over she asked me if I wanted to follow her in my car to her apartment. It was a rhetorical question to which we both knew the answer.

When we got there about twenty minutes later, we did some delicious kissing and I did some carefully methodical groping. (I was going to say petting but that always sounds stupid to me). What a strange word to use. That's what I do to my dog! "Caressing" sounds too sweet and innocent for what I was doing.

She was going along at first, but then she suddenly heard a sound from the next room and she told me she just realized her roommate was home and we had to stop. I was pretty determined so I kept trying to persuade her. I was getting pushier and pushier.

I grabbed her by the shoulders. "Who cares what the roommate thinks? Come on, we can be quiet, right? I really like you. Please!"

Suddenly she yelled, "STOP OR I WILL CALL THE POLICE!"

At first, I was mad. "How could she turn me down after all the other stuff that happened? Was she just playing me all along? What the hell's going on??? ALL THIS FOR NOTHING?"

Then I looked at her face and even through my childish rage I saw that she looked REALLY serious. Then I saw her eyes and I could tell she was terrified. It seemed unreal that it was me causing her to be afraid. It was like a bad dream. My compassion lit up and exposed my indignity.

I thought, "How could this be ME? – After all, wasn't I the good guy? - not some monster who scares women! I'm sober and I'm a helping professional for Christ sake!"

She was crying by then and said, "please leave."

She didn't have to tell me twice.

I went outside and I was shaking and fumbling with my car keys and I couldn't unlock the door, so I stopped for a minute to take a breath and it hit me….. HARD!!!

I had become the thing I hated the most. I was the goddamned 4-F guy (remember him) and the "rape her in her sleep guy" all rolled into one. I was Julian fucking Assange except the national secret I just revealed was what an asshole I was! I was even worse than them. At least maybe they never claimed to be nice guys! They didn't flaunt their compassion like a badge of entitlement.

"SHE ACTED LIKE SHE THOUGHT I WAS TRYING TO RAPE HER! COULD I REALLY DO THAT? "

I didn't like the way that question made me feel. I couldn't even blame it on booze or drugs. I told myself then and there; I NEVER want to be that guy again. NEVER EVER!!!

I managed to get in my car and probably sat there for about five minutes debating whether to go back up there to try to apologize, but my mind was clear enough by then to realize it could just make things worse. The siren that I was hearing seemed to be getting closer and it made me panic for a minute. DID she call the cops? I left in a hurry, feeling the worst shame I ever felt. I had been a little sexually aggressive before, but no one had ever felt they needed to call the police. The sirens going off in my head were worse than the real ones. No excuses, no rationalizations, just me facing the ugly, screeching truth.

I still feel shame just thinking about that night. Sometimes shame is justified and can lead to growth. It remains hard to believe that it was me, BUT IT WAS. At least it was one version of me. I wish I could find that woman someday, but I don't even remember her name. I would like to tell her that I'm deeply sorry. I'd also like to tell her that the look on her face that night and her tears helped save my life.

That night also started my real sex education. The one that happens when life finally gets your attention.

Getting Better

After my womanizing phase I was very fortunate to meet and enjoy a sexual relationship with a woman who helped me feel both sexual and less driven. She was a helping professional herself and we were very intentional and honest about our relationship. She was also incredibly multiorgasmic and being with her made me feel like the ultimate lover. In a way, that shouldn't matter but for me it did. It was a nice bonus.

What was most helpful, though was the way we were able to communicate about sex. On the very first night we met we had sex. She was hesitant, but she was very straight about her concerns. She told me that she had been on some one-night stands and she felt bad after-wards. She believed that men wouldn't ever respect her in those circumstances. She wondered if this would be another one of those bad dates. I told her that it would not affect my opinion of her and I meant it. After all, I would be doing the same thing and I don't believe in double standards. We had a very good relationship for a few months and we mutually ended it, parting as friends. Neither of us were in a hurry to make a long-term commitment.

That may have marked the first time I had an adult approach to sex. In a comfortable way, we discussed the issues and resolved them just like any other matter. It helped put sex in its place. It was civilized, sexy, and sober.

After that things got a lot better. I took dating very seriously and I was much more discrete. It wasn't long that I met the woman who has been my partner for forty years. Growing to love her was amazing and trans-formational. Mostly, I was attracted to her character and her love of peo-ple. She was attractive physically too, which made it an even easier decision.

The day I proposed to her was deeply spiritual. We were having lunch in a rather drab café with tacky décor, so I can't attribute my actions to the atmosphere. I sat there listening to her talk and basked in the light of her kindness and strength. I had no plan to form the merger, it was com-pletely spontaneous. She agreed to the idea that we would marry in a year and we left the restaurant. When we walked outside, the sun had just burst through the clouds, and I saw colors in the sky I had never seen before. I felt more alive than I could ever remember. My former divide between sex and love became imperceptible, evaporating in the warmth of the sun.

Five – The Gender Factory

"Achieving gender equality requires the engagement of women and men, girls and boys. It is everyone's responsibility." - Ban Ki-moon

Creating the Mold

Despite our alleged superior intelligence, humans aren't very good at dealing with ambiguity. Most of us like to keep it simple. During our first months of life we have choices forced upon us. What to eat, what to wear, and what to play with, are restricted. Of course, we wouldn't survive very long without these limits because babies are notorious for making bad decisions.

There are more choices to make when kids are mobile. So, parents have a job to do - keep the child alive and safe. Unfortunately, parents write their own job descriptions and pass them down like family recipes. Once safety is assured, the shaping and molding begins. Often choices children are allowed are too restricted. This is especially true as they get older – a time when they should have more autonomy, not less. "You can only go to that party if it's all boys or all girls." "You can't go out on a date because you are too young" instead of, "How can you be with that person AND address our parental concerns?"

Ambiguity is tough for some people. I'm old enough to remember a provocative TV talk show host named Joe Pine who was known to have a wooden leg. He was interviewing a rock star and asked, "You have long hair, so you must be a girl, right? The guest replied. "You have wooden leg, Joe, so you must be a table."

Cloning

Though many parents would deny it, they tend to make their children in their own image. Boys and girls are assembled from the spare parts of the parents' experience. Some want their children to be clones of them and others want their children to be a better version of them, or even opposite from them. Either way the child is compared to standards set by the parents with the parent as the reference point. While it provides parents with a blueprint, this is often not a formula for the child's self-discovery and fulfillment.

We "genderize" our children by the way we cue them and lead them. We may be more likely to play roughly with a boy, for example. This is not inherently wrong but if he objects to it we should honor that and not force it. When he was about four years old, I introduced one of my sons to a co-worker who playfully picked him up over his head and spun around. My son said in a very calm voice, "Please put me down, I'm not enjoying this." My co-worker was a bit stunned when my son simply asked for what he wanted instead of crying or protesting loudly. It's a good idea to teach kids to say 'no' right away if they object to something that pushes their boundaries. This even includes things like tickling. If the child objects; stop right away, even if they are laughing at the time. Words take precedence over body language. If body language was enough, we would not need words at all.

Separation Anxiety

Traditionally, boys have a different experience from girls, because they are biologically like their fathers, but are usually raised by their mothers. Sometimes, the boy assembly line has parts from both parents more than girls. Young boys are confused about their identity from the time they are three or so and some never overcome the confusion. When they start getting pushed away from their mothers, and they demonstrate they are sufficiently "boy", they are often allowed to explore the world with more freedom than girls.

It's a bit of a tradeoff because girls may start life with a more embedded identity and less confusion, but they are more bound to it and limited by it. They are less free or have different freedoms. Many women cannot separate themselves from their mothers during their lifetime. If they do, it may be a total break after a serious falling out. They often maintain closer ties with their bio families and they become the caregivers of aging parents. Even as adults they might get very upset if their mother or both parents show disapproval. Even many progressive-minded, working women feel this strong pull.

Boys, on the other hand, are encouraged to separate early from their caregivers and they are ridiculed or worse if they don't. Although not always the case, boys get more permission to find out who they are, and girls are assigned a fixed identity. I've never heard, "Go west, young woman, go west." When there is gender bias, he is "finding himself" but she is just "lost."

Early in life, she is charged with the task of caring for others and he is pushed to fend for himself. Later in life she may readjust and start doing more things for herself, while his maturity depends on his ability to learn to care for others. Hopefully, with enough experience, they both learn to strike a balance between caring for self and others.

I read a question on a blog recently that asked, "Is it bad parenting to give a girl the same freedom as a boy? I agreed with the blogger who advised the parent to give them "the same freedom but talk with them about the risks." Where I might disagree is what risks to emphasize. It might depend more on personality than gender per se. The child's age, location, experience, etc. might also factor in. In other words, "context sensitivity."

Beginners Luck

Even with forced separation from their mothers, boys have ample female role models because they are around females more than girls are around males. In the early school years, most teachers are women. If kids get sick they are seen by doctors, mostly men, (two-thirds of doctors are still men) but the real care is given by nurses - more often women (90% of nurses are still women). Boys are more likely to have female babysitters and traditionally have rarely been left in the care of other males for very long.

Male privilege and all its benefits are born in this sense of freedom and autonomy, but a price must be paid. He must be independent and rely mostly on his own strength and wits to guide him. He must never be afraid - or if he is, he must never show it. He must know how to do things without being taught. He must excel at the art of bullshit to cover his tracks. Most importantly, a boy must remain a boy forever if he can. He cannot grow up and become a mature adult. "Boys will be boys" is not just a cliché – it's a command. To disobey would be a betrayal of all the men that ever lived. In the sexual assault culture men are urged to cover for each other. He can fly carelessly if he has a parachute and a good "wingman."

Men are often blind to their situation and it's a mistake to think that men are to blame for having privilege. It is inherited from previous generations and cultures. For example, most of the major religions assign a lower status to women. An expression of male gratitude found its way into the beginning of a traditional Jewish prayer:

"Lord God, leader of the universe, who did [fortunately] not make me a woman....."

Not to be outdone, Christians have their own versions of conveying privilege. One is:

"Let a woman learn quietly with all submissiveness. I do not permit a woman to teach or to exercise authority over a man; rather, she is to remain quiet." 1 Timothy 2:11-12.

Islam also has its own way of underscoring male superiority:

Quran 4:34 "Men are in charge of women, because Allah hath made the one of them to excel the other, and because they spend of their property (for the support of women). So good women are the obedient, guarding in secret that which Allah hath guarded. As for those from whom ye fear rebellion, admonish them and banish them to beds apart, and scourge them."

Although we didn't create our own elevated place in society, once we are aware of it, we have a responsibility to rectify any injustices caused by it. I used to tell alcoholics that I treated that they didn't cause their disease, but they are responsible for their recovery nonetheless. Overcoming out-moded ideas about manhood is a recovery process as well.

Being a man offers advantages, but not without a heavy cost. The greatest disadvantage men have is developing the capacity for attachment and intimacy. This intimacy disability contributes to shorter life spans, more isolation, and a persistent, dreadful feeling that something crucial is missing in the lives of men. That's because it is!

One Stands Out

Role models affect our ideas of manhood. Of the most important ones, some are relatives, and some are not related all. We usually form our ideas about adulthood and gender roles from several people, not just our parents or families. Yet sometimes, for better or worse, our early impressions of manhood, womanhood, adulthood, and relationships are shaped primarily by one or two people who make an indelible mark on our psyche. It can be mothers, fathers, other relatives, teachers, coaches, etc.

My mother and my father were alcoholics. They bickered or fought frequently. They were both responsible, hard-working people, but the drinking brought a lot of drama. I have no doubt they loved each other and their children, but the love was hidden behind a protective shield in their intense battle for control. Sometimes love would burst through any way.

When my mother was fading away from cancer several years ago she had a panic attack one afternoon. She thought she was going to die immediately. She yelled to my father saying, "Earl come quickly, I have to tell you something."

Dad rushed into the bedroom and she commanded, "Sit down and you'd better listen, because I'm only going to say it once."

He sat and earnestly asked, "What is it, Rita?"

She replied, "I love you Goddammit!"

She hadn't told him that in decades and she had to think she was dying to force the words. When I heard about the incident I realized I couldn't remember them ever saying that they loved each other directly to each other. One of Mom's favorite sayings was "actions speak louder than words." I guess when we think we're on our last breath, words may be the most important actions.

How we react to good or bad role models can vary and can result in both positive and negative characteristics or tendencies in ourselves. Our early experience often creates dilemmas or tension between what we want to be and what we don't want to be. In my case, I sometimes avoided the possibility of conflict (like my parents had) by sabotaging my relationships. On the other hand, I hungered for a more positive connection than they had. I would form deep relationships quickly but when they ended, I didn't try to salvage them. I couldn't distinguish between fighting with someone and fighting for someone. I still hate conflict today, but I've learned that it's necessary sometimes.

"We are afraid to care too much, for fear that the other person does not care at all." – Eleanor Roosevelt

In my youth I had no relationships that lasted more than a few weeks. I wanted the intense connection, but I didn't want to get too attached in case the relationship turned sour. Of course, it doesn't work that way; we can't have intimacy without the risk of pain.

I had tried that attachment thing once with my favorite dog. When it died, I was devastated. After that, it only took losing a couple of girlfriends for me to figure out that loneliness was much easier than loss. Also, when I was alone there was little chance for fighting.

It was unrealistic for me to expect a healthy, intimate relationship as a teen anyway. Most teens aren't capable of real intimacy because they haven't fully formed an identity. We can't share who we are if we don't know who we are. The attempts at serious relationships by teens are more appropriately called pre-intimacy. For most people those early relationships are rehearsals for the real thing to come later. That's why, even though we aspire to be a monogamous culture, we tend to practice serial monogamy. We keep trying until (hopefully) we get it right.

Unfortunately, our culture pushes us to try serious, committed relationships at an early age. Boys are pressured to start things going which is ironic because they are probably the least qualified to lead the way. This made sense historically when young people usually established their identities by the time they were in their late teens. In generations past, relatively few people received education beyond high school and their career choices were limited. Today we are set up for failure because we get into relationships that we're not ready for, or we outgrow, and then we blame ourselves or our partner when they fail. This leaves serious emotional scars.

When I lecture about marriage I often ask the rhetorical question, "Do you think we have a high divorce rate in America?" Of course, almost all my students answer affirmatively. I then proceed to tell them that they are wrong. I explain, "If we consider marriage as an agreement between two people who truly know each other, and they each know themselves, then most married couples are not really married. They merely bought a license to cohabitate. So, we have a low marriage rate, not a high divorce rate."

As an example of an extreme non-marriage marriage, I share the story of a co-worker. She had been married for about a year and one day she went out to lunch with a friend who asked her, "How are your husband's children doing? It's was deeply embarrassing because she didn't know her husband had children. She didn't even know he had been previously married. She divorced him over this because, she said, "I felt like I had been sleeping with a complete stranger all that time." She was.

We have opportunities growing up to observe all kinds of relationships. Of course, parents affect our attitudes about them, but others can make an enormous difference, and whether we think it's fate or just good luck, the effect can be profound. I spent a lot of time at a friend's house from third grade to eighth grade. They never fought in that household, not even an argument. It was so peaceful there, but somewhat boring too. It was too much of a good thing for someone with my background. From eighth grade on I hung out with more 'interesting' people.

The Co-Parent Effect

Our early development is forged in the crucible of the nurturing and adversity we experience. Each blend is different, and each of us may duplicate the mixture of our parents or caregivers, create our own, or meld them both into the alloy of our personal world view.

Sadly, many people are not ready for the demanding role of "parent", yet they find themselves in it. Is it even possible to be fully ready for such a formidable task? Even parents who seem well-prepared are at the mercy of the unpredictability of life. It's helpful, and probably fair, to think of our parents as doing the best they can with what they have, but most parents are lacking in some way or another. Because of societal changes, even those who seem to be ideal parents may be preparing their children for a world that no longer exists. One unavoidable aspect of having two parents is the impact their interactions with each other have on their children.

Along with genetics, this observable co-parent effect is crucial to development because we depend on our caregivers to form different parts of our personalities. If our mother and father figures don't mesh, then we have conflicting parts of ourselves. To get a sense of this, imagine your parents as a figure skating duo. Would they glide across the ice together, dancing, jumping, and spinning in graceful unison, or would they collide with each other and crash to the ice in tragic disgrace. Maybe they would just be a little awkward, but you could see the determination on their faces and admire them for the effort.

MANSPLORATION: Think about your own parents for a moment and decide what kind of ice dancers they are/were. Once you identify it, how has this colored your own relationships?

Reflecting on Respecting

Respect is vital to a healthy relationship. But this issue is complicated because sometimes respect can be disguised as extreme niceness and it can be a form of conflict avoidance. Respect means assigning equal value to the other person. If conflict is open, parents can show children how to deal with it effectively. We can confront issues AND show respect.

"We don't need to share the same opinions as others, but we need to be respectful." – *Taylor Swift*

I include Taylor's quote here because she spoke out on politics recently for the first time and severe backlash ensued. She received hate mail including a tweet that said, "Shut up and sing." Despite the controversy, or maybe because of it, there was a major spike in youth voter registration. Some families avoid conflict and opt for showing a facade of cheerfulness. They shut up and smile. They become passive-aggressive.

"Silence is argument carried out by other means." *Che Guevara*

Even families with frequent and very vocal disagreements don't necessarily harm children. The key is whether they resolve the conflict or not. This includes adults admitting to each other when they are wrong, the sooner the better. Even if we disagree with a child we should own our mistakes if we turn out to be wrong. I would sometimes tell my children they couldn't do something before I had all the facts. More than once I had to change my mind. Surrendering to additional information or good reasoning is not a weakness, it's a strength. It also teaches children how to speak up for themselves. It's very beneficial to provide them with opportunities to calmly make their case, otherwise before you know it you'll have a twenty-five-year-old still throwing temper tantrums.

Couples don't have be together all the time or have similar interests or personalities to be connected. They can be good role models even if they live somewhat separate lives. It's not how much time is spent together - or even the quality of the time; it's about finding the working balance between individuality and connectedness for each couple.

A friend of mine has been married for a long time and they started their marriage with an agreement that they would have a fifteen-year trial period. At the end of that time they went out to dinner and discussed whether they wanted to continue. They both enthusiastically renewed the contract. He told me that the trick for them is that they own a duplex and they live in separate units. That doesn't stop them from being partners for life, nor does it prevent them from feeling very close. I guess you could say they keep falling in love with the one next door.

MANSPLORATION: Respect can be defined as realizing the equal worth of another person and treating them accordingly. It doesn't mean that people always agree, or even always like one another.

Using the definition above, did your parents or caregivers show respect for one another? If so, how? If not, how was this shown?

Could they ultimately resolve issues or agree to peacefully disagree?

Codes of Concealment

As a man, a counselor, and a teacher, I have learned about scenarios that created a sometimes unspoken "man code," a set of rules about male behavior and what is expected. These beliefs and attitudes begin early in life and may be relatively consistent or may yield to events and circumstances that can change our ideas throughout the lifespan. Some of us learned values as children, that we later had to shed to make personal growth possible.

Intentionally or otherwise, many boys and girls are taught to believe that if mistakes are made, then forgiveness is unlikely. Youth today have seen our country in a constant state of war and peaceful resolution of conflict may seem impossible. Feuding in the media and social media is a constant. If we have also experienced a shortage of forgiveness from our parents or society, we don't trust authority. In families where sex is highly taboo we are less likely to deal with issues that arise. Sometimes our lack of trust for authority is justified.

One of the most difficult situations I ever had to advise a student on occurred in a private Christian school. He had chosen this high school for his student-teaching because he believed there would be no behavioral problems there. After a few weeks in the classroom, he was allowed to teach without a regular teacher present. One day after class, two teen girls stayed behind. They said they had an important question for him. They said, "We think you're really cute and we would like to give you a blow job."

He pulled me aside after class the next day, seeking direction. He was concerned that the girls would be shamed by school personnel and might receive harsh consequences. He also feared that if he didn't report it they could spread rumors about him. I left the reporting decision to him but encouraged him to document everything, including his conversation with me. If he was going to report it, I suggested discussing it with the school counselor, who might be able to talk with the girls confidentially.

Secret Society

Some caregivers, intentionally or otherwise, taught secretiveness in other ways. Men are taught to keep some secrets for other men, either by direct instruction or by reactions when a secret is exposed. In college fraternities, we hear slogans like, "Bro's before Ho's." This is a man code proclamation designed to protect fraternity members from accusations from female victims of sexual assault. More basically, it normalizes the injurious behavior. We can't grow if we are hiding the truth. This conspiracy of silence and secrecy is destructive to men because it trains them to avoid revealing their true selves - the key to real intimacy and personal responsibility.

Keeping secrets for others can also lead to imitating the behavior. When I was nine or ten my Dad and my Uncle asked me to be the lookout on the stairs leading to the basement. While I watched, they exited through the window to sneak down to the local tavern after promising their wives they wouldn't go there that night. It's still a vivid image, two grown men wriggling through a small window as if they were escaping Alcatraz. I thought about how enchanting a tavern must be if they were willing to do so much just to go there. I also thought I would be the kind of man who would never sneak around or lie to his wife - one of many things I said I would never do but ended up doing.

MANSPLORATION: One section of man code identifies which secrets to keep and which not to keep. These include:

A male who is unfaithful or sexually aggressive.

Someone who is drinking or using drugs (whether underage or just hiding it).

Homosexuality or any homosexual feelings.

Any feeling that may not seem manly.

What secrets were you expected to keep? To help you with this, think about times you were either told not to tell, or someone got upset when you did.

Open Spaces
While most families or friends have secrets, some made it a point to encourage openness, even if it meant being uncomfortable. Honesty, emotional openness, inclusiveness, and diversity, are often considered to

be positive values for families and individuals. Progressive ideas about gender are not a new phenomenon. A man who grew up in the 1950's with older sisters who were assertive and successful, told me:

"I was shocked after I started school and began hearing about things boys could do and other things girls could do. MY sisters could do anything!"

So, generational differences may be more a matter of degree than a complete difference in beliefs about gender roles. Generations overlap and education level, family norms, and individual personalities, also play a role in influencing these beliefs. Millennials, although generally more flexible in their beliefs and tolerant of gender diversity, cannot bring about change alone, because they don't yet hold the reins of power.

Manhood on Display

We are taught by our caregivers and others what it means to be a "boy" or a "man." These gender scripts are modeled and etched in our minds by people who envision roles for us to play. The stage direction varies, based on culture, the era in which we were born, the unique dictates of our families, as well as other factors.

Particularly in the areas of character, demeanor, sexuality, and physical characteristics, boys are bombarded with messages - often contradictory, frustrating, and confusing. "Be manly but not macho." "Don't start a fight but be sure to finish it." "Be confident but don't show off." If those messages aren't confusing enough, just try to make sense of this one:

"It is of dangerous consequence to represent to man how near he is to the level of beasts, without showing him at the same time his greatness. It is likewise dangerous to let him see his greatness without his meanness. It is more dangerous yet to leave him

ignorant of either; but very beneficial that he should be made sensible of both." –Blaise Pascal

I agree with Pascal's premise that we need to be aware of both sides of our nature but how can young men know which side to obey in real-life situations? Most common situations don't require a beastly or great response, they just require some flexibility. The more we are restricted in our gender configuration, the more likely we are to be very bad some-times, or to appear too good to be genuine.

One of my worst displays of masculinity as a child involved serious cruelty on my part. One of my brothers was four years younger than me. We had gotten boxing gloves for Christmas and we were practicing with them one day. I hit him repeatedly and told him that "if he cried, he was not a man." I feel guilty about this and struggle with understanding where that idea of manhood came from. I don't recall a time when someone said that to me directly, but I suspect it was absorbed from many interactions. Since then I have discovered that "Big boys don't cry" but men do. I'm glad I didn't stay a big boy forever.

Gender Benders

Some cultures had fluid ideas about gender and behavior long before modern times. Various native American tribes identified and accepted several genders for males and females. When French settlers saw males, who performed duties more akin to the roles of women, they assumed they were homosexuals. They called them "berdache" which is French for male prostitute.

The natives called them "two-spirited." Although some were sexually involved with other men, that was not the basis for this alternate gender.

Some tribes had as many as sixteen different terms for genders. They were based on the functions they performed in service of tribal life.

Even these practical and creative native American tribes did not go far enough! Indeed, if gender is initially an educational process, then every individual has a unique gender. Individuals don't come out of a shared academic learning process with the exact same knowledge and beliefs, even if they attend the same school. So, it's unrealistic to think our social education produces the same result for everyone.

Father "No's" Best

One of my clients tearfully shared the painful lesson his father taught him.

"Every day for most of my childhood my dad would come home from work and I would leap over the front porch steps and fly into his arms as he approached. One day he stepped aside at the last second and my face hit the sidewalk. I looked up through a stream of blood and Dad said, "Don't take people for granted, Son. They will always disappoint you."

Most men have things to say about their fathers, either pro or con, but many men I've talked with were profoundly affected by the absence of a father figure. Comedian, Jon Stewart, has said that his parents divorced when he was eleven, and estrangement lasted until his father died. Stewart added that this was one of the reasons he started using his middle name professionally (he was born Jonathan Stuart Leibowitz). The omission was related to feelings he had about the minimal relationship with his father.

Father absence, although important, can be overrated. Single moms often do a good job of raising boys, and others can help children by being surrogate fathers for them. I remember some coaches and teachers who were great role models and it was easy to decide which ones to emulate. They provided a buffet of characteristics to choose from. It's probably more difficult to menu-select traits from your parents because there are no substitutions allowed, especially during our early childhood years.

MANSPLORATION: What images of manhood surrounded you growing up? Did they become part of your makeup? Did you consciously try to act the same or differently?

Did you have a person or people who treated you like you mattered and took you seriously?

What were you taught about trust?

One Species

Objectification is a stubborn habit. In relation to girls, boys learn early to separate gender and friendship. Alliances with the opposite sex are suspect, even for children. When I was a child, my male friends and I would call each other "girl suckers" if we spent too much time with girls.

Relating to the opposite sex in such a binary way has its costs. Later as adolescents, objectifying the opposite sex and reckless promiscuity are closely related. After all, if you have a female friend (especially one you find attractive), and you don't see her as a sex object, you may be viewed as deficient in some way. Men are taught to be opportunists and missing an opportunity is not manly.

To make it less personal, women can even be seen as inanimate objects in male lingo. Pursuing women is called "chasing skirt." Note how in the previous sentence a human being is reduced to an article of clothing. Recently we've graduated to MILFS and cougars. In the age of online live video chat and virtual reality porn, the danger of depersonalization is even greater. The last thing men need is a greater feeling they can control sexual situations without considering the needs of other people.

I counseled a college Senior after he had an affair with a married woman. When she ended it, he was totally obsessed about losing her and not at all concerned that the affair damaged her marriage and her children. I didn't offer him comfort, but I didn't shame him either. I simply said, "Life is full of opportunities to learn." He replied, "Yes, we shouldn't have met at her house the day we got caught."

Which of These is Not Unlike the Other

We have seen changes in society and a little more fluidity in roles but, by their attire, societal expectations of behavior, and prescribed roles, boys and girls are constantly reminded that they are different. I was surprised recently when I approached a classroom door loaded with instructional materials. I struggled with the doorknob while a female student watched. She waited until I opened the door for her. We don't see each other as humans because we aren't allowed to. We should though, because we are the same species after all. New norm - whoever has the lightest load should open the door. I'm amused now when I see a man opening a car door for a woman, especially when she's driving.

MANSPLORATION: How were you reminded that girls are different than boys? Were you ever teased about a friendship with a girl?

How segregated were you growing up? Did it make you shy or nervous around girls? What other effects did the segregation have?

Children of the Future

Gender differences are not inherently good or bad. Certainly, during times in history where division of labor was more necessary, these differences had utility. We can imagine that one day, a long time ago, a man and a woman approached a door of a cave or a hut at the same time. They both tried to enter and got stuck. They decided that from then on, the woman would enter first. It soon caught on and became a custom. No long conversations needed.

As time went on new customs developed and everyone forgot why they developed in the first place. Separating boys and girls and treating them differently was merely a matter of convenience (and birth control), but it became the norm. Even in their recent more disguised forms, these norms, like more subtle school dress codes, have been called into question because they no longer have a clear purpose.

There may still be some benefits for boys and girls to be segregated and to develop mostly same-sex friendship during some stages of their development, but this should not be done automatically, or just because of tradition. We should weigh the pros and cons before we make policies or rules.

Today some parents are trying to raise children in a gender-neutral way. This may become more common, but ultimately the ability of these children to thrive will depend on whether enough people see the benefits of a gender fluid society. Technology may be the great equalizer many have hope for.

The Male Milestone Mentality

When it comes to sex, many teen boys are still pressured to adopt a milestone mentality, such as getting to first base, second base, and so on (kissing petting, etc.). Of course, many girls share these goals, but boys are more likely to feel responsible for initiating the cycle.

Boys talk, and boys compare. If we look at it from a relationship perspective, this obsession with what others are doing (or not doing) misses the point entirely. Sex should be a human experience, not just a series of activities or measures of imagined maturity. This is not a moral position as much as it is a concern about how men are very late in the game when it comes to experiencing real intimacy. It matters because even if boys learn the mechanics of sex, they are often doing so at the expense of relational development. The skills required for healthy relationships are not learned by practicing sexual machinations.

The pressure on boys to act on sexual urges begins with biology, but it's heavily reliant on the quest for higher self-esteem and social status. The pressure becomes so intense that even some boys we would consider to be "good kids" become aggressive in their pursuit of a higher place in the pecking order.

Boys generally fall into one of three categories; the clueless, the vicarious, and the experienced. Let's say, for discussion sake, that each category represents about a third of all boys.

The <u>clueless types</u> are unaware of what's going on around them.

The <u>vicarious types</u> are aware and curious, but don't participate directly (even though they may wish to).

The <u>experienced types</u> are sexually active, some responsibly and some not.

While male sexual forwardness is commonplace, many teenage boys strongly disapprove of aggressive sexual behavior, yet many don't confront it. One obvious reason for the reluctance to confront this type of aggression is peer pressure. Another reason is just unfamiliarity and not knowing how to intervene. A third reason, and perhaps the most insidious, is our human tendency to admire competency. We repackage this competency drive into masculine form as achievement in as many quantifiable ways as possible, including financial and sexual. The biggest house, high-tech toys, the most exotic car, and, of course, the hottest girls, prove our competency. Sexual success is defined as sexual liaisons (or the appearance of it) with the most attractive prizes or objects. Some men want to be seen publicly with "beautiful" women even if they don't have a sexual relationship with them. One salesman told me he liked to take an escort with him to business dinners because it made him look more successful. Somewhat to my surprise, his wife thought of the idea.

The "vicarious types" are the weakest link in preventing sexual misconduct because they have mixed feelings. Secretly many boys fantasize about being wanted by girls who are "out of their league." How can they confront boys who seem to enjoy sexual success when they want the same thing at some level? Even boys who understand intellectually that womanizing is an empty pursuit, feel left out or one-upped at times. Strong envy can stifle outrage.

If a third of boys are sexually clueless and a third are experienced, then the remaining third (vicarious types) can tip the prevention scale and curtail sexual assault, if they have the incentive to do so. (A later chapter in this book will address this).

MANSPLORATION - Have you ever envied other boys for their social or sexual success? Have you ever tried to be one of them but failed? How did this feel?

If we base relationship choices on the status of the girl "object", what are the tradeoffs?

The Aggressive-Protector Duality

Girls inadvertently contribute to the male aggression dynamic in some ways. They are often attracted to boys who seem like they can protect them. We find this at the high school and college levels especially. A female freshman may attach to an older boy to feel more at ease in this unfamiliar environment. Even if she doesn't pursue this intentionally, she may be targeted by upper classmen who may exploit this vulnerability.

Aggressive boys may appear especially attractive because they can fend off any threat. This can also be true about same-sex couples where the dominate partner is in the protector role. In any relationship, if the protected half remains in the partner's good graces safety is assured.

The problem with the protector mindset is that it is automatically triggered to attack imminent threats, perceived or real. Aggressive individuals are not known for their problem-solving skills or flexibility. If the submissive partner becomes the threat, the aggressor can easily turn on them. Further, these types of relationships thwart intimacy because of the power dynamics. Aggressors are primed for battle, not for rational discussions. Besides, deep intimacy can only occur between people of equal status and power.

Some protectors don't just offer physical security, they also protect their partners' feelings. While this is comfortable at times, it allows avoidance of issues that may need to be discussed. Protectors may harbor negative feelings and instead of expressing them, they build up and explode at some point. Other protectors may do the opposite. They may frequently belittle their partners to convince them they can't make it on their own.

Wanting More

Boys and young men have sensitive feelings and want to love and be loved in a deeper sense, but they are often taught to conceal it. Some young men have accurate information about human sexuality, but that doesn't necessarily translate to relational competence or social success.

Parents who inform their children about the birds and the bees also need to help them learn how to achieve intimacy through communication and mutual consent. Along with the importance of honest self-disclosure, adolescents need to be taught that maturity means asking for what we want and accepting the answer. Social skills don't come naturally for many people, so we need to make it part of any health ed curriculum.

Consent or Assent?

"Consent" is giving permission. "Assent" goes further because it implies not just permission, but also approving of the action. Many times, people give in to things they really don't want to do, usually because they expect something in return. That's still consent but not necessarily positive. It is not always in our conscious mind, but we all do this. If we think we are doing someone a favor, we feel they should give us something. We sometimes forget that "no good deed goes unpunished." So, we could think we have full assent, but be surprised later when the person feels used or cheated.

Consent is not enough unless expectations are clear beforehand. We need to listen to that inner voice that reminds us of the importance of both men and women consenting only to interactions they really want. We must also challenge the myth that men want only sex and women want only relationships. Misunderstandings can occur and fester when we use one of those to get the other without prior disclosure.

Different Cultures

Coming of age can be an excruciating process. Boys and girls are hurt by each other because they are separated as children and taught how they are different instead of how they are alike. Interaction between males and females is a cross-cultural experience just as much as ethnicity, race, national origin, gay vs. straight, or gender fluid vs. gender rigid. Unfortunately, society hasn't recognized the need for comprehensive cultural sensitivity training for boys and girls. A deeper understanding of the experiences of developing males and females is a good start in rectifying this.

In their backyards and schoolyards boys are frequently exposed to chauvinistic and misogynistic banter and other toxic stimuli. In early adolescence, many boys adopt the milestone mentality. As mentioned earlier, they anxiously ponder that first kiss or more advanced markers of their sexual progress. They hear their peers talking about their escapades. Even though many boys exaggerate, the less experienced ones take it all in and compare themselves. If they feel too far behind they experience intense pressure to catch up.

Girl education also begins at home and in the school yard. Imagine you have something special and exciting, but you must pretend it doesn't exist. For girls, acting conspicuously sexual is taboo, yet they must appear to have sexual potential. They are taught coyness as an art. They are also brainwashed into shame. If a girl likes sex and makes it known, she is "slut-shamed." We've heard about the cruel and primitive practice of female circumcision (genital mutilation) in some third-world countries, but doesn't our culture try to accomplish the same thing with surgical-strength guilt?

So, boys must appear sexually interested and experienced, even if they don't have the actual history to strike such a pose. Conversely, girls feel they must look pretty or sexy whether they are interested in actual sexual behavior or not. Incidentally, according to the Oxford Dictionary the word "pretty" in Old English also meant "cunning" and its Germanic base meaning was "tricky".

There's a big difference between looking sexy and being sexy. Yet boys react to this 'trick with mirrors' by imagining they are the key to unlocking all this incredible suppressed sexual energy. A potent polarity indeed! The result is that she is urged to avoid responsibility for her sexuality and he feels duty-bound to assume responsibility for both, even if he is unprepared. Then at college-age, or at working age, we extract them from separate boy and girl cultures and drop them together into a foreign and complex, co-ed culture. What could possibly go wrong there?

Six – The Split Self

"Truth is everybody is going to hurt you: you just gotta find the ones worth suffering for." - Bob Marley

Because society has rigid ideas about gender - everything men and women do together can be easily sexualized. Even as children we get crazy messages about male/female friendships. One client who had relationship issues told me that when she was a little girl her mother warned her, "You are water and all men are dying of thirst." In other words, men have no control over their sexual impulses - they can't be trusted!

These kinds of messages leave little room for nonsexual bonding for males. We are a lonely lot. Further, we raise boys in a boy-culture and girls in a girl-culture. When boy meets girl (or vice versa) we don't realize it, but it's a cross-cultural experience. We don't have many workshops for cross-cultural training for men and women, but we should!

This early programming contributes to the split self, one persona that interacts with men and another persona that interacts with women. It means that the whole self cannot show up in a heterosexual relationship, or any relationship for that matter. We connect with the man or woman but not always the person. That's why so many relationships fail. The "man" and "woman" may complement each other but the two human beings are often incompatible.

The split self, combined with guilt and shame, guarantees relationship problems. One man told me that he couldn't own his sexuality because of guilt and shame. He thought he was doing something wrong if he persuaded a woman to have sex with him. He married the first woman he had sex with because his "sin" created obligation. He didn't really like her or respect her as a person, but that made it easier to have sex with her. Because, if sex is bad, who would want to do that to someone who was virtuous. For many people respect and sexiness are antithetical.

Perhaps that's also why some women go for the "bad boys." Their shame resonates with these men like a tuning fork. Others may instinctively feel protected by an aggressive male, not realizing that aggression may someday turn on them. Yet other times, these women believe they can save these men, and maybe sometimes they do. That tendency for "nice-looking" girls to like the bad boys used to bother me until I figured it out. They need each other and who am I to stand in the way?

This joke, a version of which appeared in the popular movie, "Good Will Hunting" makes the sex vs. respect point crudely yet poignantly. I had heard it years earlier from a sister-in-law:

"A couple were celebrating their tenth anniversary and she asked him what he would like for his for a gift. He told her he would like her to do something she had never done, give him oral sex. She told him no and that the idea was disgusting. Their twenty-fifth anniversary rolled around, and she asked the same question. He replied the same way pleading even harder. She admonished him to never bring it up again.

On their fortieth anniversary she asked him again. When she declined he asked why she wouldn't do it just this once. She told him that she feared he would lose respect for her. He assured her that he would never lose respect because of their long commitment to one another. She felt assured and went ahead.

The next day the phone rang, and he answered it. He turned to her and said, "Hey cocksucker, it's for you!"

This much-discussed Madonna-Whore complex is prevalent in our society. We need to become comfortable with the idea of women being sexual and not be threatened by it. In primitive times inhibiting female sexuality helped males feel assured that their children were more likely to be their own. We really don't need to stifle female sexuality because they, like us, can be sexual and think at the same time. Besides, they have the right to use their bodies how they want. Suppressing female sexuality is deeply rooted in male insecurity.

We sometimes blame female victims of sexual assaults just for being in sexual situations. This doesn't just hurt women, it hurts men too. It implies, again, that men cannot control their sexual impulses, and even worse, it robs them of compassion by lowering expectations. Men are even punished when they seem too compassionate.

My wife and I were fishing in a pond one day and I hooked a painted turtle and reeled it in. The turtle was crying and sounded like a human baby. Jane helped me take the hook out and we threw the turtle back, hoping it would survive. We caught a few fish and went home. She prepared the fish for our evening meal, just the way I like them. I couldn't eat because I was still haunted by the sound of the crying turtle. When we share this story with friends I usually get teased. I have to remind people that men can be compassionate too. One guy tried to argue that I couldn't survive with that level of sensitivity. I assured him that were I hungry enough (like we rarely are in modern society) I would eat the fish - and given no other choice - perhaps the other fisherman.

I'm fortunate and proud that my compassion muscle was developed in early childhood. One day, as a boy in Little League baseball I caught the final out of the game and was walking to the umpire to give him the ball. As I approached, I overheard him commenting about a woman in the bleachers who was noticeably pregnant. He said to the other umpires, "Wow, there's nothing like the tits on a pregnant woman."

I was so incensed that I pretended to hand him the ball and at the last second, threw it into center field, and said, "If you want it, go get it!" It just seemed so perverse to conflate breasts that would sustain life with playthings. Many years later as a college counselor I would hear frat boys refer to breasts as "fun bags." In both cases they showed how we can forget that these body parts are attached to a human being.

We act on the idea of the person-sex division without thinking. We are constantly vexed about this. Do I like this person, or do I like the package they come in? No matter how beautifully wrapped, a gift has value, only if it brings us joy or meets a positive need. When we are attracted to a person only for their looks it's like keeping the wrapping and throwing away the gift. It's not wrong, it's just self-defeating. Here's one more person we may never get to know because we inflate their value from the beginning. If we are strongly attracted, it takes longer to really know them because we want to impress them, so we don't fully self-disclose. When we are enchanted our perception is distorted. We may decide too early that they are "worth suffering for."

We may reject others out of hand because of their appearance. There are so many great people we'll never know because of first impressions. What if the love of your life is out there and he/she is suffering the same way you are, never knowing what was missed because of a blinding narrowmindedness.

We perpetuate the problem because, if someone looks good, we want them to stay that way, even if they must hurt themselves to do it. If we like what our senses capture, it's like a virtual reality camera recording. Once the video is made we want to play it repeatedly in the virtual part of our brain until it no longer stimulates us. We grow numb to that which once excited us. If we place too much importance on one dimension of a person, there is always someone better.

Our eyes sometimes betray us. At a high school party, I was dancing with a girl I liked because she was extraordinarily cute. When she wanted to dance with other boys I immediately felt hurt. I mentioned this to her friend and she said, "Just because you like her doesn't mean she has to like you." That comment seemed so obvious and inane at the time, but as a more mature man it strikes me as deep and profound.

If we look more closely, whenever we are attracted to someone it's like they have triggered something in us that demands an answer. Deep down we feel they owe us something. We have a new itch that wants to be scratched. Even the least narcissistic person can feel slighted by an unanswered look or smile. When we're under the attraction spell, we hate when it's broken, especially if it seems like the person deliberately ignores us. If we have too much of a split self, we will obsess on this, especially if we are unable to see the object as a person. We become like a dog or cat chasing a laser beam. Lasers are bright, but they only shine in one direction, and you can never really catch them.

When people have a severe split between the sexual self and the rest of the self, they can't control their sexual compulsions and "no" is the last thing they want to hear. As I write this the Bill Cosby sentence was handed down. One TV reporter mentioned the three to ten-year sentence. Another commentator discussed how Cosby was two people. In public he was a family-friendly icon and generous philanthropist, and in private, a sexual predator. She expressed surprise about this. It's not surprising at all when we look closer.

Cosby as an adult was, among other things, doing programs for children. He was desperately trying to hang on to innocence. He was trying to keep himself in an emotional straightjacket and something had to give. He was alienated from his race by not understanding black popular culture. When he admonished black youth to pull their pants up they saw the irony. "You should have kept yours up," some tweeted.

It's not hard to imagine a lot of pent up frustration and taking that out on victims. This is basic passive-aggressive behavior on steroids, driven by intense shame and anger. If someone this split has power and money, virtually anything can happen. I have had men tell me they would be afraid to have too much money because they couldn't trust themselves to control their compulsions. We see stories all the time of lottery winners who go overboard and rags-to-riches actors or athletes who end up in tatters of disgrace.

We talk of "new" money vs. "old money." The difference is that sometimes old money may have a family legacy of learning how to handle the power. Of course, old money families may have as many problems and I don't want to assume anything, because pedigrees certainly aren't guarantees. Nonetheless, not everyone can handle power or wealth. Some rich, entitled kids know they will be protected if they act out. This can finance their impulses. This may apply in the Brett Kavanagh case, and in the case of Stanford student, Brock Turner, who was arrested for sexual crimes. The Turner case was well-publicized because of the unusual circumstances of the case – his assaulting an unconscious woman near a dumpster for one thing. The case caught further attention because of the unusually lenient sentence given by the judge, who was later recalled because of it.

Those who commit sexual crimes are extremely split, but it would be a mistake to think that the rest of us aren't split, at least some of the time. Our ability to contain our natural impulses depends on both internal and external factors. Money, power, and opportunity would be included in a list of external factors. Self-esteem, self-awareness, and the ability to talk about our feelings would rank highly on the internal factor list.

Most of us get a small glimpse of the effects of the split self and rejection when we crush on someone. It's even more painful when we crush on someone over a period of time and we are relegated to the "friend zone." Think how illogical this is. We talk about the friend zone, or that person is "just" a friend as though these have less value than a sexual relationship. If we really think about it, being a friend or having a friend is wonderful, with or without sex. When we are less split we can enjoy being attracted to someone, but we can contain it and enjoy the friendship. We are connected person-to-person.

Today we have even become comfortable with the idea of "friends with benefits" which can be viable if both parties are on the same page and the page doesn't turn. Beware of the split self. It can lull you into thinking that both parties will remain friends. If either is hiding their feelings (especially from themselves), resentment will set in. Sometimes resentment gets set in stony contempt. Beware when the split self is wounded.

Even if it doesn't result in criminal behavior, the split self can ruin good friendships. But, if we are lucky, we can have a high level of attraction AND enjoy the platonic relationship. People who enjoy both probably have less shame to start with, or they have found a way to heal. They have learned to accept the split self and integrate it.

Seven – Falling In Love with Your Bad Self

"Evil is a source of moral intelligence in the sense that we need to learn from our shadow, from our dark side, in order to be good." - John Bradshaw

Gradual Growth

Despite all the growth from my feelings that day I realized I could be perceived as a sex offender, and the elation I felt when I discovered my love for Jane, the split self didn't just evaporate because of those key moments - it slowly disintegrated with the accumulation of wisdom going back to my youth.

In basic chemistry terms, it is like a suspension vs. a solution. The split self is more like a suspension, parts that will never combine totally, but when shaken they appear to be more like a solution. In the absence of occasional shaking the self will split again. At my worst point I was so emotionally disconnected from myself I became extremely reckless. I needed a severe shaking up and I got it.

Bullet Point (Trigger warning – violent act described)

In human tragedy and disaster there is redemption - if we survive to learn the lesson. During my dark period I became reckless. I went places that were unsafe, looking for adventure. I followed women into dark alleys of depravity. I had the delusion that because of my basic goodness I would be spared bad outcomes that ordinary people would face. I was a good man in a bad world. I would love lost women and help them find their way. They would pay me back by affirming my manhood and my worth. Other men would envy me and show gratitude for the lessons I could teach them. I had survived the Army, narrowly missing combat, so I could do anything. I was invincible. I had no fear. Really, I was freaking delusional and drunk half the time!

One night a couple of young men decided to show me that I wasn't in the divinely protected class I thought I was. They robbed me at gunpoint after I left a bar and they told me to hand over my wallet. I tried to grab the gun and almost did. I was quick, but not quick enough. My hand slipped off the gun and the armed one kept control with both hands. He commanded me to walk away and after I walked about fifty feet into a dark space, he shot me in the back. I felt the bullet enter and it skated around the outside of my rib cage and exited through the front of my chest. Had it bounced a quarter inch the other way, it would have entered my rib cage and destroyed vital organs.

Instinctively and instantly, I decided to act like the bullet missed. I kept walking without losing a stride. I felt that if they knew they hit me, they might feel they have to finish the job. That night, in a matter of seconds, I made a vow to myself that if I lived, I would not continue to be unhappy, and that I would devote my life to the purpose for which I was destined – to help others and to love and be loved.

The most horrible night of my life was also one of the best. When you look death in the eye and survive you have a different kind of fear, not of dying, but of not really living fully. Every breath I've taken since that night is appreciated. Every person I've ever met since then is precious, even the guys that robbed me and shot me. I got so much more out of it then they did that it almost seems unfair. Love thine enemies, but that doesn't mean I want to ever see them again. My compassion does have limits.

This incident and others not quite as dramatic had a cumulative effect. Eventually, I got sober. I left the impossible marriage. I married an amazing person. I went to grad school. I became a psychotherapist and a college professor. I became a man - a man that will never surrender his compassion no matter what! My mother was right! I was different – I was destined to be whole!

Alone, Not Lonely

Most of my epiphanies have come after dark. This has meant some sleepless nights. Sometimes it was just settling an intellectual philosophical argument with myself as a college student, but other times it was wrestling with my soul. One night during my separation, before the divorce was final, I visited my daughter who was in another state. I barely got to see her, and I had just been through a series of failed relationships. I had also lost my job a week before. Things looked bleak as I headed home. I wanted to drive the whole way, but I was too tired. I got a room in a dingy hotel and laid on the bed as soon as I settled in. Thoughts of ways to kill myself flowed through my mind like dispassionately browsing through a catalog. I started crying, whimpers bursting into heavy sobs.

I was lying on my back and suddenly and unexpectedly, I stopped crying and my arms wrapped around me as if they had their own will. The words, "I love you" occupied my head like an ear worm, repeating over and over. After a few minutes I realized that I was giving myself the compassion and love I had always reserved for others. I decided then and there that if I had to live my life alone I could do it, and I would never need another person to feel complete.

Shame can't overshadow self-love and despair cannot defeat a wise fighter.

Knockout Punch

I have always been a skillful fighter even though some thought I was a coward. My skills involved defusing the situation or using only enough force to stop my opponent. I didn't need to win a fight, I just wanted it to stop. Sometimes I was ridiculed for "backing down." In seventh grade a boy attacked me by hitting me in the stomach. He tried again, and I wrestled him to the floor and held him down until the teacher arrived to break it up. My buddies wanted me to challenge him to a fight after school but for me the issue was settled.

Much later in my mental health career I was required to restrain adolescents occasionally. Some of them were amazingly strong, especially when agitated. Some of the staff would get angry while restraining and would inflict pain on the patients. I would use just enough of my power to get the job done and talk calmly to the patient at the same time.

I was also more consistent than some of the staff. We had a method called corner confrontation where we would ask an agitated or disobedient patient to stand in a corner of the room facing that corner. The idea was that in the corner they were safe and so were we. (It also reduced their visual stimulation which can decrease agitation.) If they didn't comply with the command, we would put them in the corner as a team.

I was on vacation one week and when I returned for my evening shift the situation was chaotic. The staff, including an ex college football player, were unable to get several patients in the corner at one time. There were three very wild teens in the room when I walked in. Raising my voice just a little, I said," There are four corners in this room and I want to see only one of them empty!" Without the need for any physical contact, they each headed for a corner and stayed there until they settled down and agreed to a group session to talk about the incident.

Why could I do this alone when several others couldn't together? Because I consistently gave the patient minimum force and maximum respect. My powerful one-two combination.

Most men are under a lot of pressure to dominate and many women feel the same pressure. We need to look no further than our current president (Trump). He's a classic example of insecurity and overcompensation. Pseudo-masculinity personified. I think even many of his supporters would acknowledge this. In relation to the governing and politics these are unsettling times, but in terms of the advancement of men and women, it may represent an opportunity. We must see various examples of masculinity to help us decide who we want to be. The biography of the famed children's TV show host "Mr. Rogers" recently was released and the author said he "was a better man" after writing it. As men we can look around and choose. Each of us can create our own tapestry of manhood from the whole cloth of our values and experiences.

Other role models provide comparisons and contrasts. I'm surprised that we still have sports like ultimate fighting in our society, but we do. We have males starring in decorating shows too, celebrating the "queer eye." We see gentle giants and vicious featherweights among us. We see skilled female fighters who deserve the chance to be stupid and primitive just like their male counterparts. If men can do it so should women, although, I wish neither of them wanted to.

Our heroes and stars reflect the divisions in American culture. Adding diversity to these media stereotypes tells us that masculinity, femininity, and all genders are social constructs and efforts to categorize. Gender is not spectrum because spectrums have bands. It's an unimaginably long continuum with as many points as there are people. To prevent violence, we must recognize the depth of the challenge and the needs of people who can be very different from one another. Some believe they still need violence. We won't convince them otherwise unless we offer them alternatives that work for them

Eight – Prevention or Circumvention?

"Liberty means responsibility. That is why most men dread it." - George Bernard Shaw

Stealing Freedom

It's normal for young men and women to sometimes focus more on the desire for freedom than the need for responsibility. Youth have an innate need for at least a sense of autonomy, even if they aren't ready for the real thing.

I'm reminded of a girl I knew in high school. She came from a very wealthy family (compared to mine) and she was caught shoplifting. This was perplexing to me at the time because I knew her parents would give her everything she ever wanted. So, I posed the obvious question, "Why?" Her answer made perfect sense. She replied, "It's the first time I ever felt I accomplished something on my own."

Her behavior wasn't based on a desire to do something wrong; it was rooted in a need to do something to meet a legitimate need. We must respect this kind of motive if we want to help youth make good decisions. Except for the psychopath, there is some positive intent in everything we do. That's why I am promoting innovative ideas and terminology for prevention. We can't effectively help others by discouraging certain behaviors without providing an alternate path for getting needs met.

Effective prevention of sexual assault and relationship violence requires that we start where people are and recognize that the process we are asking them to undertake may be daunting. Essentially, we are asking them to go against their own instincts, learning, and habits. They also must defy powerful socio-cultural pressures.

"Circumvention" seems to be a good term for a more comprehensive approach towards prevention. One meaning of this word is "to anticipate and counter somebody else's plans or reactions." Designing prevention strategies or programs without anticipating these predictable counter-re-actions virtually assures ineffectiveness. People will always find ways to get needs met despite our best efforts. When they understand their own motivations, they are more likely to own these needs and find more re-sponsible ways to meet them.

One evening a few years ago I was grading a paper. As I read through it I noticed that some of the language was familiar. The more I read, the more I had a deja vu sensation. I went through some essays from two semesters earlier and found a paper with the same language (verbatim all the way through). The only difference was the name on the paper. I re-ferred both students to Honor Court.

I don't know the outcome because that is handled by the "court", but let's assume they both were required to do, let's say, some community service. Giving a punishment is designed to deter future incidences. That would be one form of prevention. Circumvention would go a step further and the court would try to determine how these two students were sus-ceptible to making this poor decision in the first place. If it was the result of the plagiarizer having deficiency in writing skills, that's one thing. If that student was working full time and it was hurting his school perfor-mance, that's another thing. Community service might worsen his situa-tion. By understanding the motivations, the Honor Court could turn the scenario into an opportunity to help the students and possibly "circum-vent" future problems.

In the Trenches

Efforts to curtail sexual misconduct must be more anticipatory than they usually are now. When you declare war on something it fights back. Consider the historic war on drugs, the war on poverty, etc. The harder we fight the more menacing these issues seem to become.

What these campaigns have in common is their shortsighted goal of changing human behavior from the outside to address immediate concerns, while neglecting to foster more self-directed long-term transformation. All externally driven prevention efforts have a shelf life, but we tend to use them beyond their expiration dates. Those working with youth who think they can do the same programs generation after generation, really don't understand adolescent and young adult development, and they underestimate the creativity and adaptivity of youth.

Case in point - the most accepted and implemented strategy to mitigate some of the effects of excessive alcohol use is the idea of the "designated driver." In theory, it assures that the one driving the car is sober, thus rendering others safer. Initially college campus groups embrace this idea and implement it forthwith. As time goes on the desire for unfettered partying kicks in and modifications are made.

As one fraternity officer told me:

"At first, we rotated the duty among the officers, then the regular members, but eventually we pushed the responsibility all the way down to pledges."

So many things could go wrong when the least experienced driver, with the least amount of authority in the group, is chauffeuring a car full of intoxicated, rowdy frat brothers!

An agonizing example of the limitations of the designated driver strategy occurred in Detroit, Michigan in 1998. After an outing, just a few days after winning the Stanley Cup, two of the Red Wings star hockey players were seriously injured in a limousine accident. One of them would never play again. They had hired a driver, so they could safely celebrate their victory. It turned out the hired driver had a drinking problem.

Just this week another limo accident in New York took twenty lives - four of them were sisters. The pain that their families must feel is beyond words. The owner of the limo service has been charged but that will never be enough to ease their suffering.

When I lecture and train students about this I often say, "If you were really serious about safety, you would have a designated drinker; one person who gets intoxicated and the rest of the group could protect him." Of course, it's said in jest, but at first, they often aren't sure if I'm kidding. The real issue is not who drives but rather how overall safety can be evaluated and assured.

Prevention efforts such as the Designated Driver are limited because they rely too heavily on social control. While this focus on peer influence is an important aspect of prevention, it must be accompanied by more emphasis on positive individual development and critical thinking.

The same is true regarding sexual assault prevention. With the passage of the Violence Against Women Act and the President's (Obama) Sexual Assault Task Force mandates - while sexual misconduct prevention efforts on campuses are required by law - success itself cannot be mandated. Recent political developments have weakened these measures anyway. That's why we need to expand our efforts, so we comply with both the letter and spirit of these calls to improve what we do. We also need to modify our approach and offer incentives to change behavior that are more in sync with today's youth.

Of course, even years before mandates, many efforts have been made on campuses to address these problems, but the results are mixed at best. Using scare tactics or guilt trips to discourage these undesired behaviors doesn't work.

"Grief is not as heavy as guilt, but it takes more away from you."
— *Veronica Roth, from Insurgent.*

It's not enough to feel just guilt; it's only when we experience grief about things we have done that we will be motivated to change. This grief sets in when we realize we were not always the good person we thought we were. One of my all-time favorite sayings (graffiti in a rest room stall of all places) was this sheer profundity:

"I thought I was better than him, and I was, until I had that thought."

Encouraging students to serve as peer monitors or interveners has probably helped; but these approaches produce a backlash effect. Probably because it is a form of guilt induction. Further, this decades-old "bystander intervention" model may be less powerful for today's youth because some researchers make the case they are "more self-centered" than previous generations. If these researchers are correct we must appeal to their self-interest to get their attention. This doesn't mean we need to abandon the bystander approach; but we do need to augment it with new approaches. These approaches will reframe the argument in terms of personal growth and life enhancement. "I want a better life" is more compelling and constant than "I want a better image as a man or woman."

Demonstrating the connection between social and individual responsibility and long-term happiness will appeal to students' wishes to make their lives more enjoyable. Yet we must make the case in a way that resonates for them to keep them set on goals that require postponing gratification in the age of the quick fix.

Circumvention then, contains both legal and social elements, but also individualized developmental elements. New, healthy social norms are generated from within. Students become self-aware enough to become willing agents of their own personal growth. To achieve a more developmentally-based approach we need to address the paralyzing orthodoxy in the prevention field. These behavioral and social problems have often been narrowly defined as "misconduct" or "criminal" behavior.

While technically correct, these viewpoints are over-simplistic because they assume the same level of intentionality in all cases, and they tend to divide students into categories of "good students" and "bad students." While there are some students who are patently immoral (just as in any population) many at the margins are coming of age, without adequate knowledge or support. They are acting without forethought because they lack a clear roadmap and the gear to navigate the steep, winding path that ascends to relational competence and fulfillment.

To some prevention staff, the remedy for problem behaviors is to make more rules and enforce them more consistently. Others believe the answer is to inform students about the down side while ignoring the short-term benefits of these behaviors and why they persist. Yet others want to deploy armies of do-gooders to stop the scourge of bad behavior by blocking and shaming their misguided peers.

Programs, movements, and changing social norms aren't enough. We also are dealing with very different individual personalities. Rules and policies, though necessary, will not stop the risk-takers, the rule benders and breakers who only feed on the exciting, high-stakes of defying prohibitions. They won't help the loner who is bumbling his way to adult relationships either. One man told me:

"I was a lone wolf. I didn't go along with the pack. Their attitudes about women were disgusting. But in the end, my hunting instinct was just as vicious. I was like the noble aborigine who apologizes to his prey, just before he devours them."

Others, while not generally rebellious or loners, are developmentally and relationally challenged and are trying to reach social and sexual milestones without the skills to do so safely. They are reliant on others to set their compass, so they follow the crowd. They need to be able to chart their own course, and it's our job to help them do it.

Many experienced Preventionists will tell you that there are three groups in any population, each with unique needs:

1.   Those who will offend no matter what we do because they are immersed in a lifestyle or are addicted/dependent. Some of these are intransigent criminal types, but many may be reachable/treatable.

2.   Those who won't offend because they are developmentally ahead of some of their peers or are just too constrained by fear or inhibitions.

3.   Those who might offend because they are developmentally challenged and/or are susceptible to negative peer culture but would gladly opt out if they had an alternative.

The best way to enjoy quantitative and qualitative success is to reach all these groups, but especially the third group; helping them learn about themselves and why they feel pressures that may lead to impulsive decisions. This group can go either way, and this is where we can have the most direct preventive impact. They're ripe for learning self-regulated growth. This kind of growth can only be achieved by developing internal controls.

Developmental theorists, including Lawrence Kohlberg and James Marcia, make the case that internalized values are more stable and persistent than externalized, borrowed values. In fact, Kohlberg considered our level of moral development to be directly proportional to how much we have accepted our beliefs as our own.

Interestingly, we are even beginning to look at the issue of peer pressure differently too. Lawrence Steinberg, known for his work related to understanding the "peer effect," has uncovered an interesting phenomenon. In an experiment to measure this effect he and his colleagues found no difference in behavior when peers were physically present to influence actions vs. when the subject believed that peers may be observing from another room. This strongly suggests that, at least to some extent, the peer effect is internal.

I once treated a young woman in an inpatient alcohol and drug program. She told us in a group therapy session that she started using drugs in the tenth grade and her parents found out. They switched her from a public school to a private school hoping this would help. She told us that she could get more and "better" drugs in the private school so it made things worse. Her tendency to seek out drug users was already established, so a change in environment wouldn't matter.

If we accept this idea, then it's a game changer. It means we must understand, and help students understand what drives them, so we can help them become the primary agents of their own psycho-social wellness. This can best be achieved through comprehensive developmental education.

"The pride of youth is in strength and beauty, the pride of old age is in discretion."
Democritus – 460 BC – 370 BC

Uneven Development

Modern youth have much more raw information and freedom than ever before, so they need even more help with discretion. Yet, they don't have to wait for old age to become wiser. This is true for some more than others because human development is asynchronous. This means that we develop in various ways at different rates. It's essential that student affairs personnel understand the full implications of this.

For example, by the time they enter college, some students may be academically ahead of their peers but socially underdeveloped. They either get lost in the system or make up for lost time by spending virtually all of their energy enjoying new freedoms. The reverse is also common as we see many students who spend a lot more time on school work to catch up to or stay ahead of the competition, but they neglect their social lives.

Others are ready for college academically and have even enjoyed social success in protected settings, but lack sufficient coping skills to function independently in unfamiliar surroundings. They lag behind in emotional development.

I recall one student who came to me in tears. She had been "popular" from grade school all the way through high school. She was now on a college campus and at the three-month mark she hadn't made a single friend. After further inquiry I learned that she had gone to school with the same group of friends all her life to that point. So, even though she was generally social, she lacked one important skill – how to find and develop new friendships. Once I pointed this out as a skill deficit instead of something wrong with her, she started joining some of the campus groups I recommended. Within a few weeks she was very pleased with her social life. I simply helped her see that she was delayed in one developmental sub-area and that was enough to address her immediate problem. We then went to work on her coping skills so that she could weather the next storm when it hit.

Indeed, virtually everyone probably has some areas of development that are out of sync with other areas, and with their same-aged peers. Students would have better chances at success if we identified these developmental deficits on the front end of their college experience.

Remember the students I sent to Honor Court for plagiarizing? They both had developmental delays. The person who wrote the paper was behind socially. He attached himself to the other student who was a popular football player. This gave him access to a social life. The football player was underdeveloped academically, so he got help with his classwork. He seemed to have enough intelligence; he had just not been academically challenged at his high school because he was a star player. They were drawn to each other because they had complementary developmental delays.

If a high number of students are arriving at college with uneven development, then we are negligent not to address this. Complicating the picture even more, some students arrive in their first year with histories of alcohol or drug problems or mental illness. Even those who lack a substance abuse history may have difficult personal issues or college adjustment problems, and they are especially vulnerable to using alcohol or drugs to medicate or mask their conditions.

Nine – College Try

"If you want to get laid, go to college. If you want an education, go to the library."
Frank Zappa

Prevention of sexual misconduct is a tricky business. When students start college, they are coming of age and some are continuing an experiment with sex and relationships that started in high school. Other students may just be beginning. College personnel try not to be intrusive for some good reasons and some not so good reasons. They are right to offer autonomy to students since it shows respect for the abilities of young adults. Mature, until proven immature. It's good for students to have to make their own decisions and learn from them. Yet, some students are ready to do that, and other are not.

If a student is engaging in sexual behavior, it's not a concern of Student Affairs personnel unless it poses a health or safety risk to the student or others. In a humorous way (addressing the issue of oral sex) J. Edgar Hoover, the famous former FBI Director, made a similar point by saying:

"I regret to say that we in the FBI are powerless to act in issues of oral-genital intimacy, unless it interferes with interstate commerce."

Unfortunately, some students are at risk on day one and colleges don't have strong enough radar to detect their vulnerability in time. Not all students have the same level of readiness and a one-size-fits-all approach doesn't work. They may be ready academically but may be behind in their emotional and social development. They need to be assessed on their ability to deal with this new environment since they spend more time out of class than in class. Much of the time is unstructured. Some are easy prey for predators. Some are potential perpetrators.

Schools have tried hard to address this, but they want to attract students, and let's face it, if word gets out that a university is strict about drinking, partying, etc., students may choose other schools. The Bill and Melinda Gates Foundation names "socializing too much" as the number two reason students fail (running out of money is number one). Lists of good party schools are online in abundance and students read them. Besides, just being strict about partying doesn't usually work anyway.

Because of funding shortages colleges must compete for students and they offer perks to attract them. The money issue is paramount because with high attrition rates, students who leave must be replaced. Like the teen with dating success, and me at one point in my life, some colleges are "lowering their standards to get their numbers up."

The emotional and social development of students is under-appreciated as a factor in college failure and sexual misconduct. I made the same miscalculation as a college counselor when I first started.

When I first began counseling students, I took the standard analytical approach because that was my training. After a couple of years, I began to feel I wasn't getting through to them. Many would attend a few sessions and leave counseling. It was a bit confusing because things always seemed to get off to a good start. I struggled with this for several months until I had an epiphany while lecturing in my then-new adolescent-development class.

I was introducing the class to the concept of "asynchrony" in human development, and the idea I was teaching them finally made sense in the real world. Wow! Those counseling clients, and virtually all students who were having difficulty in college, seemed to have one thing in common: They were out of sync with their own development.

I reviewed many cases and saw the same pattern—one or more areas of developmental imbalance. Many students had social problems. They were either socializing too much (with so much newfound freedom) to make up for lost time, or they would study excessively and not socialize enough. Either way, many ended up leaving college or transferring because they failed academically or felt isolated and lonely.

Once I saw the patterns, I came to see that on the first day students enter college, many are in a developmental crisis. I realized that all students should be assessed in several areas, including their social skills, and emotional readiness. These would not be tests to find mental illness; they would be self-assessments to evaluate where THEY see their vulnerabilities and need for growth. The results of these assessments would be used to identify the types of support they will need to adjust and succeed.

This data and interviews with the student can lead to a learning contract between the student and the institution. Participation should be voluntary, but students who opt out would be required to sign a waiver stating they were informed about any concerns and offered appropriate services. This individualized approach would bolster many students and increase their chances for academic and social success.

The lack of assessment on the front end, hampers prevention efforts dramatically. EARLY INTERVENTION IS ALWAYS BETTER. Going after misconduct when it's happening is good but it's better to stop it before it starts. As I recently wrote as a guest blogger on the Psychology today website:

"Those who think they can program and proselytize youth into persistent behavioral change really don't understand adolescent and young adult development. They don't understand primary prevention either; which attempts to eliminate the need for sexual misconduct before it happens.

Due to the nationwide scourge of sexual assault and intense pressure from advocacy groups, prevention measures in public colleges are required by the U.S. government and many private schools are voluntarily doing prevention programs. Though efforts can be mandated, success cannot. To be successful we must anticipate the likely responses to prevention methods and have a deeper understanding of today's youth.

Using scare tactics or guilt trips to discourage these undesired behaviors has limited effect, partly because youth believe, 'it will never happen to me.' In addition, these methods often backfire because they insult the intelligence of students - they already know the dangers, but they still feel compelled to navigate complex social situations for which they may be unprepared.

The popular bystander intervention approach is secondary prevention aimed at stopping behavior while it's happening. Encouraging students to serve as peer interveners has helped; but this approach can produce a serious backlash effect. The pejorative term 'cockblocker' has become part of the lexicon on many campuses for a reason. It speaks to the entitlement that many young men believe they possess, and their anger when it's challenged.

They need to be shown that this entitlement does not exist, and that it's as toxic for them as it is for others. We should harvest the lessons from past anti-cigarette smoking campaigns, which only became effective once more smokers were convinced by hard data that they were harming themselves.

The more recent 'social norming' approach makes a strong appeal to youth who are prone to social conformity, but it may have less effect on others. Social norming involves disseminating information such as, "95% of students don't mistreat their partners." Although it qualifies as primary prevention, it may only reinforce existing positive behavior. It is unlikely to change current or future negative behavior, especially once it becomes habitual.

Unfortunately, all these methods can be even less compelling for today's youth because they may be more egocentric than previous generations, and egocentrism tends to accelerate during the transition to college for many students. If these researchers are correct, we must appeal to students' self-interest to get better results. We must also make the case in a way that shows them the more immediate benefits of treating sex as an interpersonal process, not just a pleasure-seeking activity or a way to gain social status. In other words, sexual development must be in sync with positive social and emotional development.

We can accomplish these goals by teaching positive personal and social development concepts. These are not just psychology or sociology lessons; they could be covered in courses in all departments - such as the Business Department offering a course on 'The Cost of Sexism in the Modern Workplace.'

Students need to understand the personal developmental pressures they are experiencing as well to minimize the possibility of autopiloting their way into trouble. With more developmentally-focused education, the backlash effect will diminish because the battle will be more internalized and new norms will be more widely embraced. While peer intervention, social norming, and discipline can support the process, developmental education will sustain it because individual self-awareness and self-interest form the crucible where long-lasting change is forged."

Home Remedies

College is a student's transitional home. College level sex education should be provided for all students. Today, many primary and secondary schools are limited in resources, and in what they can do for political reasons. Like it or not, when one level of education falls short, the next level must make up for it.

I had one student (a Senior) ask me if it was true that "gay men have different anatomy and nerve endings in their anus." I told her that this area of the body is an erogenous zone for everyone and some people are more interested in that kind of stimulation, both male and female." I wasn't sure of the purpose of the question, but it was a good opportunity to inform the class and debunk an inaccurate sexual belief. Students generally showed a high level of interest in learning about sexual health.

Occasionally, my wife, a registered nurse, would sub for me and teach my class about "adolescent health issues." Since this was extra material they wouldn't be tested on, she told them they didn't have to take notes. She told me that despite this, they took notes furiously when she got to the section on sexual health.

College sex ed should include the physical aspects of sex, but also healthy relational skills and sexual ethics as parts of the curriculum. It should also be a safe space for students to talk openly. In the classroom, students should be protected from harassment or ridicule by other students, regardless of their personal choices, but we shouldn't shy away from talking about it. It's crucial for administration, student affairs personnel, and faculty to create a firewall around the students who are different from the majority, and those who are victims or perpetrators when incidents are alleged.

Of course, sexual labeling by others or name-calling should be prohibited, and we need to react swiftly when it does occur. While sexual minority students should be protected, the long-term goal should be integration into the larger community when and if they want that.

Again, we are essentially addressing cross-cultural educational needs. Groups designed to bring women and men together for serious discussion break down stereotypes. Gay/straight dialog is just as important. Relationship skills training groups could help everyone.

We also need to proactively teach tolerance and help students appreciate the complexities of human sexual and relational development. We can provide environments that reject shame-based approaches to preventing misconduct. Most importantly, we must show young people how seeing others as objects facilitates misconduct and interferes with intimacy, and ultimately, their personal development.

It's essential that we men face our outdated views about sex as a phenomenon separate from relational considerations. We have been brainwashed into thinking sex as an end-in-itself will somehow do things it really cannot do; make us whole or make up for the life-demands placed on us. Some men still think something like, "We work, we go to war, we protect our families, we help make babies, and that entitles us to a reward. Women are well-equipped to provide our consolation prize."

Nowadays there is no guarantee we will do any of those things and no person should be an award or trophy for another. In the future we may not even be needed for reproduction. The MeToo message is, "Hey buddy, wake up. You are no longer a privileged class, and we are trying to help you adjust." As men, we can accept the help graciously or fight it, but there will be discomfort and pain either way.

Emily Linden, a well-known women's and victim's advocate recently made a statement saying that she's not concerned if some innocent men get hurt in the quest for women's justice. She is right in that there is always collateral damage in a war. The mistake we could make is to think that women have declared war on men. The "enemy' is the mistreatment of vulnerable people, including men, when it applies.

Sean Penn recently argues that "nuance" is lacking in the MeToo movement. Of course it is! We can't reverse generations of abuse without being loud, clear, and persistent.

My answer is to get men and women and lock them in a room together until they work this out (not a literal lock, but a structured situation). There are more good meal delivery options today in case it takes a while. If they really want to bring about change they would focus on how they ALL contribute to the problem.

Keep the Change

Change is hard. When I was in grad school I joined a men's group. Several of the guys were attending school and their wives or partners were working to support them. Even though it made perfect sense for these guys to do more housework, they struggled with this because they felt un-masculine. Even today I talk to young men and some feel bad if they are unemployed and not the breadwinner. Even if their spouse makes more money than them they are bothered (very irrational since it brings more resources to the household).

Why do the archaic ideas persist? Usually for one of two reasons; 1) They just don't philosophically buy into the concept of gender neutrality or equality; or 2) They are insecure about their masculinity.

Some may not even like to do traditional "male" things, but they feel they must keep up the image. It just doesn't make sense to do things you don't like, especially if you don't really have to.

My partner in life, Jane and I divide chores based on what we each like to do. She likes cooking; I enjoy cleaning. (OK, "like" and "enjoy" might be overstated, but we don't mind it.) Whatever is left, we negotiate. If we get bored or too busy to do the agreed-upon chores, we negotiate. If we argue about it we either renegotiate, or we decide it isn't worth arguing about.

The same is true with sex with one caveat. People should never have to do anything sexually that they don't want to do. If you want something, ask for it. If you get a "no", you can negotiate. If you still get a "no", it's time to stop. If you argue about it, you will damage your relationship. We don't have the right to demand sexual favors from anyone. Sex is not a mere chore, even if it feels like it sometimes. We have the right to set our own limits; it's a basic human right.

Some of the male tendency to want sex on demand is biological. He fears that he won't be able to perform, so "ready or not here I come", is his declaration, and sometimes his practice. This is only a problem if we define sex as having one goal, intercourse with ejaculation. There is a whole spectrum of things we can do without having intercourse. Once couples adjust to sex as a continuum of possibilities that can be stopped and started at any point in the process, they become more mutually accommodating, and they have much less stress. Forced agreements don't hold anyway. In some cases, couples could just agree to disagree, but that means they should both be ready to stop bringing it up.

Jane does not like it if I open a food item when a similar option is available. For instance, if I open a new box of breakfast cereal, and there are other kinds of cereal opened and already in storage containers, she gets upset. We only have so many containers and she doesn't like open boxes sitting around for various reasons. That's fine – I don't judge her about that. Nonetheless, when I want a certain type of cereal, that's what I want. I don't even negotiate this because I know from past experience that if I get hungry in the middle of the night, and I want a certain cereal brand, I will get it. It wouldn't matter if I agreed 12 hours earlier not to do it. There are just some things I won't compromise on, even for the person who is most important to me in the world.

It's different with sex. Pertaining to it, we have to agree and abide by the agreement. The difference between sex and breakfast cereal is that (although they're both great in the morning and at night) only one requires consent. I have never needed to hear an affirmative "snap, crackle, or pop" to feel comfortable eating my cereal.

Ten – Justice Delayed

"Foolish people inflict pain upon them self which is worse than what an enemy can bring upon." _ Thiruvalluvar, Thirukkural

Compulsive behavior is outside of awareness by definition. I once had a friend who was on a diet and we were at a party where they had one of her favorite appetizers, stuffed mushrooms. She asked me to help keep count of how many she ate. At the end of the evening we compared notes. She believed she ate three, but I stopped counting at seven! This is not to suggest that compulsive eating and sexual misconduct are equivalents, but the dynamics are similar.

In a way, men are set up. Not by women, but by the mindsets that men and women are programmed to adopt. Boys learn a script which compels them to seek a progression in sexual activities in the beginning (first base, second base, etc. or kissing, petting, and so on). Later they may consider completion of the sex act a necessity. Sex can become addictive like mushrooms. We can lose count and think we haven't had enough, or we haven't gone far enough.

The same kind of mindlessness ended the senate career of Al Franken. He left the Senate after it was revealed he had groped some women in the past. He had been a staunch, and I believe sincere, advocate for women's rights and progressive policies in general, but that wasn't enough to save his Senate seat. I believe, even though redemption is a painful process, he will be better off in the long run because he did not engage in a drawn-out fight at the expense of his constituents. He will have the opportunity to reflect and grow.

The issue came up on Bill Maher's popular HBO show in September of 2018 and Bill took the position that the reaction to Franken's behavior was extreme and that the behavior was no worse than that of others who had gotten away with it. Michelle Goldberg, a reporter from the New York Times, was a guest on the show and she interrupted Bill's monolog to object to his characterization of Franken's behavior as "not that serious." This was an awkward moment and Bill called her "out of place" for talking during the closing monolog.

This ugly cable TV spat exemplifies the difficulty of knowing where to draw the line when it involves sexual assault. Grabbing breasts and buttocks is definitely assault, but is it enough to end someone's career or send them to prison? Does the context matter? It's a thorny problem because I think both sides have a point.

Sexual assault is a crime. Period. Ruining careers or lives could be wrong in some circumstances too. Was Bill justified to question the response to Franken's behavior? Yes. Was Michelle justified to be concerned about Bill's criticism of that response, even if it meant interrupting a scripted part of the show? Without a doubt.

If we reduced some types of sexual assault to misdemeanors as Germaine Greer suggested (groping, no threats or weapons, etc.) it may result in more convictions, but the deterrent effect of the law might be weakened. It also might cause people to take sexual assault less seriously. Further, if we can argue that men (or some of them) are less accountable because their culture has predisposed them to sexual misbehavior, then we also need to accept that women are more predisposed to serious psychological damage because of the same culture. And, it's not just cultural for women; it's also based on the actual threat level, which involves fear of being killed or physically harmed, pregnancy, STI's, etc. It's not fair for men to get some slack, while women get the same level of pain and suffering.

As a 35-year-old Texas woman said about outdated laws:

"There's a gap here where it doesn't matter if someone forcibly shoves their hand between my legs. They say it's like disturbing the peace, but it's disturbing more than the peace. It's violating."

Perhaps the how-serious-is-it controversy exists because sexual assault is different from other forms of assault. If we hit someone or push someone there is physical danger, a bruise, fall, etc. If we grab someone in a sexual way, the harm may not be visible, but the psychological damage may be severe. My then ten-year-old son taught me a lesson once about walking in another person's shoes. He got a scrape after a bicycle fall and it seemed minor to me, so I told him that he would be fine, so there was no need to cry. (Yes, I know! Bad parenting - but I was in a hurry.) He looked me in the eye and said, "Dad, you don't know my pain." We simply can't know the level of suffering of another person by outward appearances.

A man can't completely know a woman's pain either. In the Senate hearings on the Brett Kavanaugh nomination to the Supreme Court, Christine Blasey-Ford testified about his alleged sexual misconduct. Kavanaugh testified on the same day, declaring his innocence. Her critics said that, even if it's true, something that long ago should be disregarded saying, "Everyone does things when they're young." Her supporters said that the effects of these incidents can be life-long for victims and this should be considered. Each side accused the other of being "political" which, of course they were. They were fighting tooth and nail for a crucial court post that has implications for generations of Americans. I'm not surprised about the tactics of either side since so much was at stake. All the politicians and pundits whining about the unfair process by the other side was a waste of time. We were on war footing.

Dirty politics aside, as much as anything else, the hearings were a slugfest over the issue of who controls a woman's body. It is not surprising that Kavanaugh was supported by the religious right because he was perceived as a safe bet on the issue of opposing abortion. Ironically, he was accused by Dr. Ford of literally controlling a woman's body and putting his hand over her mouth to silence her. Whether it's about the right to choose or sexual assault, the battle cry of backward-looking men and women is "Deny, deny, deny." Denial of facts or rights never works for very long because we can't run away from reality no matter how hard we try.

Sadly, everyone loses no matter who seems to win in an end-justifies-the-means war. One of the biggest losers is Kavanaugh himself. If any of the accounts of his youthful experiences are true, he has some serious problems and he is not overcoming them. Like all of us, he needs to own his problems, or they will own him. Since he did get confirmation, everything he does on the Supreme court will now be viewed as partisan and dubious. The Supreme Court itself is now compromised. Their motto is, "Equal Justice Under Law." After this Senate fiasco many women are feeling that this doesn't apply to them.

Some groups are leveraging the fears of men and racial minorities for political gain. One conservative group, asserting that MeToo has gone too far, did an ad claiming that liberals will cause blacks to be lynched if they are accused of assaulting a white woman. They cite the Kavanagh hearings as an example of overreach. They have become confused about the concept of "innocent until proven guilty." This standard only applies in criminal proceedings. All other legal actions have a lower bar such as "preponderance of evidence." The Kavanaugh hearings were not a criminal proceeding so this claim of a rights violation is a red herring.

We might also wonder how Kavanaugh could claim to be a virgin until adulthood, and yet be accused of sexual assault as a teen. It's not that difficult to speculate that he had a lot of pressure and pent up frustration. His "work hard – play hard" mindset left little room for self-reflection. He also may have had guilt and shame about sex due to his religious upbringing, so he couldn't act sexual when sober. He was a good Catholic boy by day, and a ticking timebomb at night. He may have made several attempts to have sex, but they failed because he was too drunk.

I understand this since I have a similar background. Although I was never as violent as he is alleged to have been, I can relate to the shame and having to be drunk to be sexual in my youth. As Shakespeare said about alcohol, "It provokes the desire, but it takes away the performance." Perhaps, because of shame and intense pressure, Kavanaugh exploded occasionally and those around him took shrapnel. The "devil's triangle" that he and Mark Judge perpetrated could have been a serious attempt at sexual assault or two clumsy, drunken boys attempting to impress their friends. Either way it would be an assault and it clearly affected the victim in profound ways.

Shame blows up after too many beers. People get hurt.

Running Scared

As men, many of us are squeamish because the MeToo movement may remind us of things we did in our youth, and we wouldn't want them to be resurrected and come back to haunt us. That's a very understandable fear. Yet, helping victims and survivors find justice is better for everyone in the long run. We should initially take them at their word if they say they are harmed by men's actions. We would expect the same if we were victims. We should also tell the truth. I think Kavanaugh's fatal flaw is not that he made mistakes, but that he didn't own them and learn from them. As Frederick Douglas wisely said:

"It is easier to build strong children than to repair broken men."

He also grew up in a privileged class. The problem with privilege is that it inhibits real growth. If we are broken and privileged, we are held together by the gravity of the status quo. It holds us together, but it also holds us down. We can only expand quantitatively, not qualitatively.

Privilege for me wasn't bestowed by money, it was ordained because of being a male, especially the first-born male. As a young adult, keeping up the image meant getting better jobs and more money. Personal growth was usually secondary. I have some regrets that I didn't take more time for self-reflection and to do a better job of balancing career and family. We all would have benefitted if I had embraced a more relaxed view of life. My vision of manhood at the time blinded me to my personal failings. I occasionally verbally abused my wife and kids because sometimes they were in the way of my ideal successful man image. They didn't make me look good enough. Of course, at the time I wasn't self-aware enough to see what was igniting this explosive mix.

Privilege and success may cause us to push our children too hard to get them to perform. We forget they need to develop internal motivation, often through their failures. I talked to a middle school student within the past few months who was getting tutoring on Algebra during the summer. Both his parents are high achievers. I asked him if he struggles with math generally and his answer surprised me. He told me he got an "A" when he took the Algebra class, but he got a "B" on his final exam. His father wasn't satisfied with this less than perfect performance, so he arranged tutoring. Maybe setting such a high standard will result in excellence, but it might cause too much pressure. This example shows how hard it is to be a parent and a child. Perfectionism can lead to excellence or chronic disappointment. I guess we need to have perfectionism in moderation. Parenting likewise, especially of teens, is a contradiction in terms.

Not Fair

Collectively, men have disadvantaged women even if that wasn't the primary goal. For example, when a man accepts a position for which a woman is better or equally qualified, he is contributing to injustice. His shortcomings are more likely to be overlooked than hers. At one point in my career, I was highly recruited for administrative positions in the private sector simply because I was a male in the mental health field. This ended up being a negative because I had a couple of positions for which I was not ready. Those experiences made me feel incompetent and the stress was unbearable. After that, by being more selective about jobs, I fared much better, even though I sometimes made less money. Peace of mind is a valuable perk.

We benefit when justice is served in the bedroom and the board room because we will be more comfortable in our roles, and because women and men will be more able to trust each other in general. It will allow us to have better relationships at home, the office, etc. At this point in history male/female relations are fractured and need to be mended. That won't happen if we are on the defensive or tenaciously hold on to power whether we deserve it or not. This includes no longer expecting women to be silent about sexual abuses.

Recently some companies have decided that the answer to MeToo is for men to avoid women on the job as much as possible. This is not only ineffective, it's a step backward. A better approach would train men and women how to work together more effectively.

Eleven – Becoming Woke

"I had a dream that I was awake and I woke up to find myself asleep."
- Stan Laurel

As a man I cannot know exactly what it feels like to be a woman who has been sexually assaulted. However, I know what it feels like to be groped, because it happened to me once as a twenty-something. I was buying shoes and the salesman grabbed my crotch after sliding a shoe on my foot. I was stunned, so I didn't do or say anything. The shoe didn't fit so I sent him back to the stock room to get another one. While he was gone I had time to process what had happened. I decided that I would let it go but, if he tried it again, he would feel the wrath of my fist in his face.

After that experience, there is no way I can fault women for the outrage they feel about what has happened to them so many times. With only one minor instance of groping, I was willing to immediately elevate it to a crime that deserved extreme physical punishment.

In reflection, I feel good about that incident for two reasons. I gave him a second chance so my merciful side prevailed, but I also had a healthy anger that was ready to bring him to swift justice. It seems to me, that we have let women down. We deprive them of a sense of justice and criticize them for even needing it. It's foolish to think they wouldn't resent this and make us pay in other ways. Although false accusations of sexual assault are rare, mistrust and hostility between men and women may be at an all-time high.

Don't Be a Hater

A case could be made that sexual assaults are hate crimes. If we assault someone only because they are a woman, or a man, or homosexual, etc. it's the same as attacking someone for being a member of an ethnic minority. A national law that treats sexual crimes as (bias-motivated) hate crimes might settle the debate about misdemeanor vs. felony. Since hate crimes have more options in sentencing than similar crimes, they might provide us with more flexibility to make the punishment fit even if some cases are charged as misdemeanors. If you're not convinced, try to think of it this way. If it's not a hate crime, imagine how you would feel if someone you didn't even know assaulted you just because you are a male.

In contrast, if I get in a fight with someone I know, it is usually followed by some reflection, and I may realize I have played a part in it. But if I'm minding my own business and someone does something violent or invasive to me there's no ambiguity. I'm not going to spend a lot of time wondering if that shoe salesman would have left me alone if I hadn't worn tight jeans that day. In fact, I don't even know or care what I was wearing that day.

Simply put, a hate crime amounts to punishing someone for just being born. Being born a woman is not a matter of choice but woman-haters don't consider that. If you still don't think hatred for women is pervasive in our culture, consider this:

'What's the worst possible thing you can call a woman? Don't hold back, now. You're probably thinking of words like slut, whore, bitch, cunt (I told you not to hold back!), skank.

Okay, now, what are the worst things you can call a guy? Fag, girl, bitch, pussy. I've even heard the term 'mangina.'

Notice anything? The worst thing you can call a girl is a girl. The worst thing you can call a guy is a girl. Being a woman is the ultimate insult. Now tell me that's not royally fucked up."
— Jessica Valenti, Full Frontal Feminism

It seems to me that any sexual assault committed by a stranger is clearly a hate crime. Sexual crimes committed in the context of relationships are more complex and perhaps a restorative justice approach makes more sense in some cases. This involves attempting to undo the harm or prevent future harm. Victim and perpetrator are brought face to face with a trained facilitator. This gives the victim a chance to confront the perpetrator, so they can convey the magnitude of the harm done. Compensation could be negotiated, and/or mediation could establish boundaries and expectations for the future. Sometimes mediation is done without bringing the parties physically together, with the mediator shuttling back and forth until agreement is reached. This spares the victim from being retraumatized. A plan is then worked out to resolve the issues and help the parties avoid each other in the future.

Getting people to own their wrongdoings is affirming. I once took some patients from an alcoholism treatment center on a shopping trip and one of them stole some clothes and jewelry from a department store. I did not discover this until we got back to the facility. I gave her an ultimatum of either returning the merchandize and admit what she had done to the store manager or leave our facility and face the court which had referred her to treatment. She was very angry with me, but she agreed to return the merchandize. Instead of pressing charges the manger thanked her for being honest about it. His forgiveness profoundly affected her and her whole attitude about treatment changed for the better.

I've had other cases where mediation produces results. One guy had slapped his significant other for the first time and she called the police. She declined to have him charged but she feared it could happen again. We negotiated an agreement wherein she would end the relationship if it happened again. I told them that that was not sufficient because they also needed a plan for what would happen when he was angry. He agreed that if he felt like hitting her he would leave and cool down and she agreed to go along with this when he used a code word. The one he chose was "mad max."

A study I once read suggested that when men are angry they feel a need to act and they want to disconnect or attack. Women are more likely to want to stay connected even if the interaction is uncomfortable. In the study men would try to leave when a conflict occurred, and women would follow them out the door. This makes sense in that women are more relational, and the threat of disconnection may be greater for them. Men are more goal fixated and want resolution or escape. Of course, there are many exceptions but in the case of the-above couple it applied and worked well.

Thinking Hard

Another obstacle, besides an ineffective legal system that prevents women from getting justice, is the myth that men can't control themselves once they are aroused. I know this is a fallacy because I am a father. When I talk to young men I assure them that they can stop at any point in the process. I describe an illustrative scene:

"And guys, I also know as a man that we can stop at any time, no matter how "turned on" we might be. I'm married, and I had small children. I have heard the pitter patter of little feet coming down the hall at inconvenient times. Sometimes you have to

stop, and you have to think quick…. But we can think and be aroused at the same time."

I go on:

Curious child. 'Hey Daddy, what's that sticking up under the covers.'

Quick thinking Dad. 'That's a book holder, Honey. Daddy likes to read in bed sometimes.'

One time a student asked, 'Well, what do you do if you're coming when they walk in?'

Another student retorted, 'Then you have to think even faster!"

Besides feeling they should get a pass if they are stimulated, men are often competitive about stats. Some compare sexual conquests like batting averages. Striking out brings shame. I don't believe this "Casey at the Bat" level of tension is necessarily innate, but it's reinforced in our culture. A friend of my son was asked by his frustrated peers why he was so successful at getting so many girls to date him and sleep with him. His response was, "Sometimes you have to lower your standards to get your numbers up."

The Modesty Mindset

Many girls are programmed with a modesty mindset which causes them to avoid showing overt signs of sexual interest and talking about it is still somewhat taboo, even today. She must not initiate, she can only react. She cannot set parameters in advance because this might mean losing a boy she likes by breaking the spell, or even worse, revealing that she thinks about sex. She may believe she has to keep him guessing. This is achieved by looking like she might be highly sexual, even if she isn't interested. It's the flip side of male posturing. She brings contrived befuddlement and he brings contrived self-confidence. She's not usually consciously trying to "tease" him and he's not usually consciously trying to deceive her, it's an automatic balancing mechanism. It's a dance routine they learn while growing up. Shame loves to dance.

We tend to be biased against girls who look sexy or attractive, both pro and con. Attractive girls may enjoy the halo effect, which means they are seen as more attention-worthy and more interesting than "plain" girls. Conversely, some observers believe they are being manipulative, intentionally seductive, or teasing boys.

I have worked with women who tell me it's the opposite. They are not seeking an advantage, they just don't want to be out of the running, just like boys. Or, sometimes even simpler - they just like the way they look! Since they are so often shamed about their bodies or looks this need for self-appreciation and affirmation from others is not surprising.

Men often need that too but maybe not as conspicuously. Fashion trends can mean one thing to the viewer but mean another thing to the wearer. Skimpier garments may affect the viewer in a sexual way, but it's the viewer who adds that meaning. It's like how two people can look at the same painting and see something completely different. Sometimes dressing sexy is expressing our freedom, or we just don't want to look too uptight. I struggle with this every time I decide whether to button my top shirt button or not. In most business situations I'm more buttoned up. If I want to have fun or be flirty I go wild and unbutton that top button. That's one reason I love t-shirts – no decision required.

I have participated in so called, "Slut Walks." These are marches that started in reaction to a Police Chief speaking at a major conference in New York saying that a victim would have been less likely to be raped if she had dressed "more appropriately." The marches involve people dressing like "sluts" and disseminating information about sexual crimes and prevention. I didn't don a slutty outfit, but I carried a sign my partner and I created. It said, "If dressing sexy means you want to be raped, then wearing a wetsuit means you want to be eaten by a shark!"

Next time, I might wear an actual wet suit.

Good girl – Bad Girl

Obligatory modesty, while appropriate in some circumstances, can segregate boys and girls even further. A high school student told me that girls in her seventh-grade class saw a movie about menstruation at school. The boys asked them about it and only one girl broke ranks and talked about it with the boys. The other girls "freaked out" when she did that and shunned her for a while. They should have made her Class President, or at least the Ambassador to Boy World.

Appearing modest and being modest is very different. True modesty is an attitude not a costume. I attended a United Way Christmas party a few nights ago and noticed the wide variety of how people were dressed. I played a game with myself to try to figure out who was an official of the United Way versus guests and people who were just there to party. I spoke to one man and said, "You look like the official greeter, dressed up but not too much." He responded by saying, "I'm not connected to the organization. Tonight, I'm the official drinker because the booze is free."

I chatted briefly with a woman I knew who was dressed in a short dress with cleavage showing. I said, "You look all decked out ready to party down." She said, "Not really, I've been working all day and I had to rush home and change. My boss said I had to attend this. This is the only dress I had that was clean."

So, choice of attire can be deliberate to elicit a response, or random, depending on the situation. We should never assume. Not only our physical appearance within our gender, but even gender itself is not monolithic or reliably predictive of personal characteristics. Embedded, thoughtless cultural norms and beliefs, produce barriers to dialog for people who are gendered differently. Even adults have difficulty discussing issues across gender lines, so youth are at the mercy of these unnecessary communication barriers until we mature as a society and show them the way. Guesswork doesn't work anymore.

If we can't judge a book by its cover then how can we expect to know a person's level of sexual interest without at least reading the foreword. We need a whole new paradigm for social and sexual interaction. The debate about how to deal with the complexities of sexual improprieties will only be resolved if people of good faith come together. Efforts are under way to begin the process of teaching healthy relationships even in the early grades.

An acquaintance of mine has co-founded a company called "Before We Begin." Its flagship product, BeYou, is an interactive, customizable web platform and mobile application that teaches kids concepts such as consent, bystander intervention, healthy relationships, and much more.

BeYou takes a holistic approach to education by incorporating the parent, the child, and the educator. Children have access to games, comics, videos and other engaging material that teaches unit content. They can ask probing questions through a search-engine tool and are encouraged to journal after each unit. Parents can access resources and materials that help them host and navigate conversations with their child.

Efforts like BeYou are a good start. We must also retrofit young adults with these concepts and establish new norms for them. Colleges have tried many approaches but only recently has the idea emerged that we need to teach healthy relationships as a set of developmental issues and skills. I have been advocating this for fifteen years. Finally I heard this echoed two weeks ago by another professional, a presenter from Everfi, an organization that assists educational institutions in improving campus life.

Fifteen long years - that's about the average amount of time it takes innovative ideas to become mainstream!

For these programs to work both men and women need to be on board. To the extent that we are in a war between the sexes and genders, we can find a path to harmony. We can find optimal solutions, but it will require dialog and open-mindedness. It's time for honesty. It's time for peace talks.

Shameless Sex Ed

In our society we talk about sex a lot, but we don't really talk about it seriously for fear it will encourage youth to experiment more. When we talk openly about sex it doesn't encourage sex, it encourages talking. A healthy dialog in any setting or sex education curriculum should be free of shame and scare tactics. By high school it should address and discourage the sexist mindsets of students. It should not be sex-negative nor sex-positive. It should be sex-neutral, but relationship-positive. In other words, besides information about human sexuality, it should contain instruction on communication, consent, and checking frequently to be clear about our partner's take on things. "Are you OK with this?" may be the sexiest thing we can utter.

Sex Ed should instill the idea that everyone is responsible for what they do, and no one should feel obligated to meet another person's desires or needs. The emphasis should be on sex as an interpersonal process that requires complete honesty on both sides. Reducing shame makes it less likely that youth will have to drink or act impulsively in order to be sexual. It's not the shame after we do something that causes misbehavior, it's the shame before we do it that all but guarantees it.

Valentine's Sway

Romantic gestures as a means of wooing someone to be sexual should be discouraged. Intentional lying or manipulation is even worse. Youth need to learn that responsible sex means that they must ask for what they want before they do anything. Then, they need to accept the answer. This makes invisible boundaries more detectable and reduces the odds of making wrong assumptions.

I recall a high school incident which caused me to shed blood. I was in a rock band and one of the band members broke up with his girlfriend. Within a week I asked her out and we went on a double date. We parked, and after a few kisses, I fondled her breasts outside her sweater. She didn't say anything, but I didn't want to go further with other people in the car. I knew this was being "fast" for a first date, but I was truly afraid she would think I was immature if I didn't try at least something.

The next night I ran into her ex and, without any warning, he punched me in the nose. I interpreted it then that he was just jealous, but now I realize he may have been upset that I had violated someone he cared about. I didn't retaliate because I thought I might be in the wrong.

This whole thing could have been avoided with a simple request for permission to touch her. Sometimes we think a frank discussion will spoil the experience. I ended up with a bloody nose that said otherwise.

Keep it Clean

When my current partner (wife) and I had been dating for a while, one evening we took a bath together. It was the most intimate we had been up to that point. I asked her if this meant we were going to have sex afterwards. She said, "No, but we will sleep better after a bath." We did. A warm bath and eliminating guesswork relaxes the body and quiets the mind.

I was almost in my mid-thirties by then, after a lot of craziness in my twenties and early thirties. I had acquired some patience by the time I met her. Patience is a lesson I've had to learn repeatedly throughout my life. Some of us are in a hurry because we fear that we will never have enough. Before my thirties I could never have enough women, beer, or food. I had to seize every opportunity like there was no tomorrow. The contrast between my second and third decade of life is remarkable. No - astounding!

Presidential Pardon

The word grace is beautiful in both its meanings. One meaning is elegance and refinement. Another meaning is that life (or God) will provide what we need without considering whether we deserve it or not. Viewing the world as a place that will always provide what we need is hard when we are deprived or damaged early in life. Postponing gratification is out of the question.

I got a lesson in grace from an unexpected source. I crossed paths with president Jimmy Carter twice in my life. The first time I was twenty-nine years old (at least chronologically.) My wife at the time and I were invited to his inauguration (including tickets to the Inaugural Ball) because my sister was married to a congressman. We were just out of college and had very little money. She had to buy a dress at the local K-mart and sew some appliques on it because that's all we could afford. I had to rent a tuxedo for the ball and borrow an overcoat to withstand the cold January Washington DC weather.

Despite the humble origin of our garments, we got more praise than the other couples who attended dinner before the ball. We were with a group of elites, with Paris-original gowns and expensive tuxes. We stood out in our grace and elegance, at least until we got very drunk. My wife became ill and had to go back to the apartment, but I went on to the ball with a group. One of the people in the group was a woman I attended college with, who worked in Washington DC. I had every intention of hooking up with her if the chance arose. I got so drunk by the time we reached the ball that I got it in my head that I would try to dance with the First Lady.

Fortunately, President and Mrs. Carter had already finished their ceremonial dance and left before we got there. The only dance I would have gotten would have been with the Secret Service, who would have waltzed me out of there in a hurry. I woke up the next morning with a terrible hangover and a profound feeling of dread. I was ashamed that I turned the honor of a presidential invitation into a dishonorable drunken spree. I had no idea then that I would meet the Carters again one day in very different circumstances.

Fast-forward about twenty years. I'm living a sober life by then. We took a family trip to Plains Georgia to celebrate my in-law's anniversary. We stayed in a bed and breakfast, and the next morning we attended the Sunday School class where President Carter was giving the lesson that day. We arrived a little late, so we went to the front pew which was still empty.

Just before the lesson started two Secret Service agents ushered Rosalynn Carter in, and asked us to find a place in the back so she could sit in the front row. She shooed them away and told them to leave us where we were. She joined us in the pew. Then Jimmy came in and started to speak. After a brief introduction, he announced that he needed to inform us that he had a policy of not giving autographs before or after the lesson because he didn't believe it was appropriate to do so at a church. My thirteen-year-old daughter was sitting between my wife, Jane, and Rosalynn. I saw my daughter's chin drop because she had a post card in hand, ready for his signature. Without saying a word, Mrs. Carter discretely reached over and took the post card from my daughter's hand, signed it, and handed it back.

We took a family picture with the Carters after Sunday School. My daughter beamed all the way home and for days after. The lesson Jimmy taught that day in Sunday School was on the topic of "hope." The lesson Rosalynn taught that day by her actions was "grace" – the kind that makes hope possible.

Twelve – Reality, Romance, and Rape

"We could not field a big enough force to avoid this risk [of rape]. We would need so many soldiers because our women are so beautiful."- Silvio Berlusconi, Circa 2008

We live in a rape culture that is like a three-legged stool. Sexism, like the-above quote, is one of the legs, and the others are antipathy and sociopathy. Romance is the seat of the stool and we can sit up straight or lose our balance. Romance in and of itself isn't a bad thing, but intense romantic feelings produce an altered state of mind that colors our perception. When we are "struck" with someone we are less likely to remain objective. If we lose too much objectivity, we become infatuated (positive sexism), afraid (negative sexism), or angry (misogyny). We predominantly feel one of these emotions depending on our personal histories. How far we go in acting on these feelings is related to our psychological makeup. This is often tied to how early in life rejection or smothering occurs. These two opposite poles determine how strongly we react to the power of women.

This spreads through the culture because men who feel that women have too much power over them tend to feel less outrage over others' misogyny, and sexual violence (because they consciously or unconsciously see it as balancing power). This is very similar to how we feel when something bad happens to a political foe even if we are generally a caring person.

These men can't tolerate feeling any more powerless than they already feel, so they don't actively challenge the rape mentality. They may not harm women directly, but they ignore, or even facilitate, misogyny. When we associate a group with negative feelings we avoid or attack. This group avoids, the rapist attacks, but the underlying feelings are similar.

It's a common belief that rape is related to a need for power and control. The question is, "Power and control over what?" While stranger rapes and serial acquaintance rapes are driven by criminal impulses and mental illness, many less violent assaults are driven by social and emotional problems. The common denominators are fear of rejection or fear of smothering, and primitive needs to prevent either. The person committing the rape is speaking in actions that translate to, "You can't say no if I don't ask", or "I will control you before you can overwhelm me." In effect, "We are connected whether YOU want to be or not because you make me feel something I don't like." People who feel overly rejected or blocked should heed the wisdom in the quote below:

"I believe that rejection is a blessing because it's the universe's way of telling you that there's something better out there." - Michelle Phan

At a lower level, the same dynamic plays out in a different way when couples argue or fight. Some of them fight just so they feel they're still connected. Bad breath is better than no breath at all. Making up after a fight is simply a way of affirming the reconnection. Make-up sex is intense, but it doesn't solve the long-term problem.

Those who feel more smothered, compulsively need to feel release or be in control. They may have had early caregivers or other relationships where they felt overpowered or suffocated. In healthy parenting or healthy relationships, we need to follow this advice:

"Don't smother [a child or] each other. No one can grow in the shade." - Leo Buscaglia

People who feel overpowered or extremely neglected will avoid or hurt others. They are unfed, trapped animals, looking for any way out they can find. This was expressed starkly by an inmate in a jail where I was a counselor early in my career. He had been arrested for a violent sexual assault and I was sent to evaluate whether he would hurt, or get hurt by, other inmates. What he said was telling and frightening:

"When I see a woman alone I can't breathe. I have to stop her from having control over me. She makes me want her. It's her fault. When I'm done with her I feel free for a while. No one controls me at that moment.

I can't look at her afterwards, because she might look at me like it's my fault."

While these extreme emotional problems lead to violence, milder forms can affect more normal relationships. Real love demands that we find the fault within.

Reality-based Love

Even in drama-free relationships, positive feelings may wax and wane, or dissolve altogether. Some, like author John Bradshaw, have said that love is not a feeling; it's a decision. Reality-based love involves both feelings and decisions.

We must feel enough love, often enough, to make it sustainable, yet we must ride out times when it doesn't feel good. That requires a conscious decision which is made many times. Judith Viorst said one advantage of marriage is that:

"When you fall out of love with him or he falls out of love with you, it keeps you together until you fall in love again."

With or without marriage, the bonds of attachment can stretch pretty far before they break. Marriage was created to assure stability in relationships, but some couples find other ways of achieving stability. Relationships can last longer if both parties were truly ready when the relationship formed. We must be self-aware to be relationship-ready. This could involve a conscious effort or just plain luck.

I feel more on the lucky side because I did everything I could to screw up my relational life, but I turned out to be happy anyway. My version of "ready" happened TO me. I didn't cause it. Because of random events, my stubborn mind finally got the point that I had to accept my life as it is. I had to start looking around me instead of beyond me. Some might argue that some divine force was at work, and I can't deny the possibility, but I don't worry about that. I accept my life, and if I'm guilty of ingratitude to some higher power, I will accept the consequences of that too.

Love and happiness depend on giving up the idea that we were supposed to have a different life. News flash!!! Nobody stole your life, even if you were switched at birth. It's all part of your life. We are stuck with the life we have right now, at this moment. The only thing we can do is adjust our attitude. We can make decisions that will change our path, but we can't hack away the path that's already underfoot, or we will stumble and drop.

This attitude adjustment has another step. We also need to accept that what happens to us is neither good nor bad, but how we react to it can enhance our lives or make them worse. That's all we can do - but it's enough.

Our feelings about money and power show how we can think something is good, but it can be bad and vice versa. If I had been wealthier in my drinking days I might not be here. If I were poor now I might not have the healthcare I need. But what if I WERE poor now? I would have to overcome my pride and ask for help. That can't happen if I feel too ashamed. Shame eclipses humility.

I have pondered the meaning of the story of the Garden of Eden many times. Even though I'm not religious, I believe there is value in thinking about what these ancient writers were saying. I have concluded that the creation story was written to contain a message for children and a different message for adults. The message for children is "obedience." Follow your parents' advice or bad things will happen to you. For children this is consistent with their level of cognitive development.

The adult message is much more sophisticated. The forbidden fruit is a metaphor for overthinking. This fruit is often described as the product of the Tree of the Knowledge of Good and Evil, but to think that God wouldn't want us to know the difference between right and wrong is silly. When you consider that the consequence Adam and Eve received for disobeying was to be cast out of paradise it makes more sense. On the surface, the punishment is way too harsh for eating a piece of fruit.

Looking deeper, I believe the author of the creation story was trying to warn us that if we spend too much time judging things that happen as good or bad FOR US we will have constant anxiety. (The electric power went out – that's bad. We lit candles, and my wife and I had the best talk we've had in years – that's good. While we were talking she told me she wants a divorce – that's bad. We finally agreed to see a marriage counselor – that's good.) I think you see the point, if we interpret events too quickly as either good or bad our lives will be full of angst. Paradise lost, one minute at a time. Shame is also a theme in the creation story. When they were ejected from the garden they needed to hide their nakedness. They became self-conscious, producing even more anxiety.

Last year a woman posted on Facebook about her high school years to reach out to girls who were struggling. She gave me permission to include it here. It's a nice piece for girls, but also an image for men to see through the lens of a woman looking back on her teen anxieties and frustrations:

"This is a message to all the teenage girls out there. First off, I am so sorry you are going through this right now. I wouldn't wish a second adolescence on my worst enemy. The good news is adolescence is a condition that isn't terminal, and it is even possible to get through it without any lasting damage. You might even look back in ten years and (gasp) miss it! Here are a few tips to get through the hardest part of your life, so you can move on to bigger and better things.

You are gorgeous. Yeah, you! Ten to fifteen years from now you will look back and wish you had appreciated the way you look now. It's ok though, because by then youthful beauty will have faded into the kind of confident beauty that comes when you are finally able to appreciate and love yourself the way you are.

The girls (and guys) who don't like you now probably won't even matter at all in ten years. If they do, it's because as you got older and more mature, you found out that you have stuff in common after all. They might even end up being your best friend or husband one day. Life is really random like that.

It is never your job to make guys not want you. They are responsible for their own actions. That said, a self-defense class never hurt anyone. If you don't want to take a class, remember that a knee to the groin and two fingers to the eyes are a very good deterrent.

I'm sorry to be the bearer of bad news, but your parents are right. It is important to try to get good grades. You may not have any interest in college right now, but one day you might. You are too young to do anything now that will limit your chances when you're older. Plus, it's always nice to be able to go to college for free, and good grades are your best shot at that. Your parents are exaggerating a little though when they say a couple of bad grades are the end of the world. If you keep up most of your grades, your GPA will even out in the end, and most schools will let you retake a class for a better grade. So, don't sweat that Pre-Calc grade too much.

That guy who is just so amazing and that you love so much will more than likely not be in your life in a couple of years. Sometimes it might take a little time to get over that, but in five to ten years, you will wonder what the hell you were even thinking. If you guys do end up getting married and living happily ever after, congratulations! Most high school relationships don't make it. And remember, if it is truly meant to be, he will wait until you are ready to be physical, and he will wait until you can both responsibly discuss and obtain a reliable form of birth control.

How will you know if you're ready? My mom once answered this question for one of my cousins thirty years ago by saying, "Don't do anything you wouldn't want talked about in the locker room." I am going to update that for the 2000's and say, "Don't do anything you wouldn't want to end up on Facebook."

I'm going to repeat it again. Don't do anything you wouldn't want to end up on Facebook. And that's not just in dating relationships. That's all the time. If you feel the need to make a few youthful mistakes, confiscate everyone's cell phones and put them in a lock box first. That way at least no one can prove it if they post something about you.

Don't drink and drive. You may think your parents will be mad and ground you forever if you call them asking for a ride home. I guarantee they will be happier about that than if they get two police officers knocking on the door in the middle of the night to tell them you didn't ask for a ride home. Plus, your parents can't really ground you forever. They just say that to scare you, I promise.

If you ever feel depressed or feel like suicide is the only option, tell someone. If they don't take you seriously, tell someone else. Someone will listen to you if you need to talk. There are plenty of resources available to help, whether this is a temporary period of being sad or overwhelmed or if it's the start of major depression. Either way, there is help available, and just like with the drinking and driving, your parents won't be mad if you ask for that help. I promise that they just want you to be happy, healthy, and safe.

Finally, have a little fun. There's a lot of scary things for young people these days to deal with, but there are still plenty of ways to have fun without making mistakes that might last a life time. Enjoy your friends. Volunteer at an animal shelter or nursing home. Read. Have movie marathons with your girlfriends. Try to learn an instrument. Go to school dances. They may be a little lame, but they are safe and chaperoned...and you might even secretly look back on them fondly. Most of all, laugh a lot.

Life is too short to take everything so seriously. Don't worry. You are going to get through this just fine!" - Hilary Evans

The above woman-to-girl advice shows mature thinking and the capacity to overcome suffering, but teens shouldn't always have to suffer to acquire wisdom. Pain is not always necessary for gain. Developmental education and understanding cultural influences are the antidotes for some suffering. That doesn't mean youth won't have problems, but it does mean they will understand more about what is happening to them and they will know they are not alone.

It also takes longer to absorb good information than bad information so the earlier, the better. When I worked with troubled youth I noticed that they often didn't seem to be listening when I was trying to explain life lessons to them. Then a few months later I would overhear them repeating what I had said to another youth, almost verbatim.

Outing Rape Culture

To protect youth from too much trial and error in socializing and dating, we should explain rape culture and how it evolved. We pretend to raise our young to behave appropriately and respect the boundaries of others, but we don't. Recently, in a brainstorming session with college students about how to prevent sexual assault, I gave an example of a typical dating ritual that constitutes sexual assault but is rarely treated as such:

"When in the presence of a potential sex partner it is common to touch them without asking permission. A young man fondles the breast of his date or acquaintance. She may push his hand away or tell him not to repeat the action, but technically, he has already sexually assaulted her. The same would be true if she touched him without asking."

Consensus on this wasn't easy to reach and most students thought the scenario was within the bounds of customary dating behavior. One student agreed with me, but said, "You're right, but how can we explain that to a high school or college student without sounding crazy?" He identified the main problem with normative behavior; it becomes invisible!

My presentation on this topic includes a PowerPoint slide of a cartoon. It shows a cave man dragging a girl from her cave with her parents waving goodbye. The caption has the parents saying, "Be sure to have her home by midnight." They don't notice the boy dragging her by the hair because it's the cultural norm of the time. Violence in this case was accepted by cave dwellers (of course, it's a cliché but it makes the point). Today we would not consider it OK to drag someone by the hair.

Once behavior becomes invisible, pushing the cultural reset button seems unnatural and extreme! If this type of ritualized behavior didn't exist, a dating scenario might go something like this:

Person #1 asks, "May I touch your breast?"

Person #2 replies, "One of them, or both?"

Person #1 – "Both, I guess."

Person #2 – "Do you mean touch or squeeze?"

Person #1 – "Both, I guess."

Person #2 – "How long were you planning to do this?"

Person #1 – "A few minutes I suppose."

Person #2 – "What do you want from this?"

Person #1 – "I just want to know what they feel like."

Person #2 – "Is this an experiment for Biology class?"

Of course, the above dialog is absurd, but somewhere between absurdity and assault is a reasonable, proactive conversation that could establish boundaries without cultural scripts or games.

Sexual curiosity and desire are compelling forces and not inherently unhealthy. In the context of a rape culture, however, they become incredibly destructive. When a university fraternity (true story) sends out an e-mail survey asking, "Who on campus would you like to rape?", we see curiosity infused with deep violence and hostility. The outrage over this incident focused on a few young men behaving badly. The spotlight should have been on whatever is happening in our society that makes them harbor this level of insensitivity and allows them to think - even for a moment - this is acceptable behavior.

Restated, the question could be, "What other cultural anomaly besides ritualistic approaches to human sexuality contributes to the thoughtlessness associated with the rape mindset?" At the top of my list would be the invention of "gender" and its worming its way into our collective psyche. To be clear, "Male or Female" are usually biological realities, but "Man or Woman, Boy or Girl," are social constructs. The marketplace loves this contrived diversity and profits from exaggerating the differences through beauty product sales, clothes, etc. Some even use rape themes. One of many examples:

A Belvedere Vodka ad shows a man grabbing a woman and the caption says:

"Unlike some people, Belvedere always goes down easy."

Although other ads may be subtler, the point is the same. Buy our product and you will get women.

A Matter of Convenience

Another advantage of these gender constructs lies in the efficiency of not having to negotiate every interaction between males and females (no ten-minute discussions about who should open the door, etc.). But efficiency is not always the best way and many people today rebel against these conventions. Objectification and categorization of people serve a worthwhile purpose at times, but gender as a guide to expected behavior is beginning to outlive its usefulness. Further, gender-based biases and rituals inhibit or prevent conversation and mutual understanding. The quote below, although sexist, does describe the way men feel sometimes:

"Because women mistakenly believe that a man should already know what they want – and they think it doesn't count if you have to tell them – most men will not know how to succeed with them." – Allison Armstrong

Years ago, I spent a few of my "single" years in Ann Arbor, Michigan and socialized frequently and sometimes "dated." I was a more traditional male at the time. Because Ann Arbor has a high number of committed feminists per capita, I could never be sure if offering to pay for the date would offend my companion or not offering would offend.

Once I became comfortable with asking - to my delight - I received the bonus of learning a lot about the person very quickly. Frank, effective communication is a healthy type of speed dating. It helps us learn important things about a person before we form an emotional attachment. We have all seen how emotions and hormones can cloud our judgment. Choosing partners is too serious to rely solely on a fluttering heart, flowing juices, or outdated conventions.

Our culture further enables this avoidance of real intimacy by promoting the idea that males and females are so different, they cannot possibly understand each other. Why bother with dialog if it will only lead to confusion, anxiety, conflict, and possibly animus?

"Between men and women there is no friendship possible. There is passion, enmity, worship, love, but no friendship." - Oscar Wilde

Although it takes time and effort to have conversations, it's better than not having them and being frustrated, and sometimes seriously harmed by miscommunication. The challenge is that when we choose to take this more open and direct approach it moves us outside the comfort of our gender roles. This can be a buzzkill at times. This even applies to same sex relationships. Object-A meets object-B is less risky than person-A meets person-B. As objects we can always fall back on "they're not my type." But ALL humans are our type for the most part!

I talked to a young woman who was a clerk in a hardware store the other day. She was short, obese, and plain looking. I started joking with her and in a few seconds, I discovered she was incredibly witty, intelligent, and well-read. I thought, "What's a person like you doing in a place like this?" I imagined that she would be delightful to have an extended conversation with. Since I'm a serial conversationalist, she is my "type", even though there would be no chance for a sexual relationship (not because of her looks, but because I am committed).

I had another delightful experience a couple of years ago. I was in an auto parts store and I was in line at the cashier's station and I got into a conversation with a teen who had just had her hair clipped to fuzz length. She had multiple tattoos and piercings, but it all seemed to fit her so well. I told her that I thought the haircut looked good on her. I saw the clerk, an older woman, roll her eyes.

The girl surprised me and asked me if I wanted to rub her head.

I did!

There was no way I was going to miss a chance to rub a fresh fuzzy head! By then the clerk seemed totally freaked out. This teen and I had just shared a special moment. We had affirmed our basic goodness and humanity and celebrated her authenticity together. Unlike the girl I dated as a teen - I rubbed HER the RIGHT way. Even though I was a conventional looking older man, she could see my innocence beam shining brightly. She was also my type – an earthling.

If we focus on "types" of people instead of waiting until we know them better, we can fall into the trap of thinking we know them and being way off. If we are genuine and a little patient, we might find out that they are different than we thought, and they may have potential to become a good friend or partner. Conversely, love-at-first-site can dissolve into dis-enchantment-at-every-sight, when they eventually show who they are. We need to be aware of exactly to what we are drawn.

"When we fall in love at a glance, the question we should ask ourselves (and this would apply to both men and women) is, "What is it that we long for? Or perhaps, what are we lacking so that we can turn life in the direction we want? Creativity? Confidence? Authority? Recklessness? Irresponsibility? Or even darkness? Perhaps the lover is the outlaw in ourselves we don't quite have the nerve to claim. (p. 34)"
   — Rosemary Sullivan, Labyrinth of Desire: Women, Passion, and Romantic Ob-session

Obsessive attraction to "types" can turn into serious romanticizing or sexual acting out. Males or females with high insecurity levels about their role performance as men or women need confirmation of this and will go to any length to get it. They are out to prove something! Thus, they ma-nipulate, harass, seduce, or assault their way into temporary feelings of safe conformity to their idealized self-concepts. One client told me that he was married but he became obsessed with a woman at work. He knew she would be attending a football game one Saturday, so he borrowed some money to pay a pilot to fly over the stadium with a banner declaring his love. He told me he almost went bankrupt because of those kinds of expenditures. Emotionally, he already was.

Social Insecurity Checks

Men who are insecure may try to prove their manhood by conquests over women or dominance over other men. Some may see fatherhood as the ultimate evidence. Women who are insecure may prove their womanhood by being hyper-feminine, dating many men, or by becoming mothers. It's no surprise that in an era where parenthood is being postponed for many people, we see a proliferation in pet ownership. Those parental caregiving urges must be expressed somehow. All the-above activities, are normal (dating, sex, and parenthood) but doing them for the wrong reasons rarely turns out well. So, whether you're in love with a man or woman, a human of any other gender, or even a dog or cat - keep your eyes shut and your mind wide open.

Fade In

"The sound of a kiss is not so loud as that of a cannon, but its echo lasts a great deal longer." - Oliver Wendell Holmes, Sr.

Choosing partners is serious business whether we are looking for a brief sexual tryst, someone to date, or a candidate for a long-term relationship. The more we know about others, the better are our chances of finding a good match. My F.A.D.E. model, represented by the diagram below, illustrates a way to make objective evaluations of people and our reactions to them without being too mechanical about it:

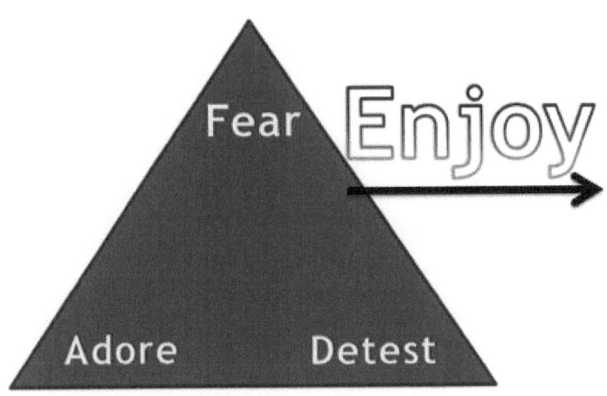

The acronym, F.A.D.E. stands for Fear, Adore, Detest, or Enjoy.

If we are afraid (fear) of a person when we first meet them, or if we put them on a pedestal (adore) or we dislike (detest) them; we cannot maintain clarity as we size them up for relationship potential. We must monitor our perceptions and manage our emotions as we make important decisions about any future involvement with them (enjoy). We must also be very certain of our needs and agenda. Among the things to avoid:

1) Infatuation – If we get excited or light up when we see another person we often interpret it as only a positive. Careful - we think they are "hot," therefore we could get burned. We are vulnerable because we give them too much power, and not necessarily because they deserve it. If our first impression is too strong it may override other information that is relevant. We need to wait until we are calm before we draw any conclusions. It's good to see them in more than one kind of situation before we proceed.

2)   Fear – If we feel uncomfortable with someone there is often good reason. Other times it's something from our past that interferes with getting to know this person. One man told me he almost missed out on his current good marriage because she had the same profession as his first wife and that was enough to give him pause. The problem lies in the fact that when we are hurt in a relationship we over generalize to protect ourselves, just like protecting a physical wound. We can be cautious but keep an open mind.

3)   Anger or Detesting – If we are angry at someone from our past or angry at ourselves we can make hasty judgments about others. We will try to avoid some new acquaintances, attack them or push them away. We can sometimes generalize anger to the point that we can be angry at all men, all women, or all members of a certain class. If we have anger issues, we need to resolve these before we seek new intimate relationships.

4)   Idealizing - If we walk into a situation looking for our ideal man or woman we are already in trouble, even if that ideal is broader than just physical attraction. I have a friend who has been married several times, twice in the brief time I have known her. Both times she described her new partners as "dreams come true." My take is that she was so fixated on an ideal of a perfect marriage, she deluded herself into thinking she had found it. The last husband turned out to be possessive and violent. Everyone saw this ahead of time but her.

The F.A.D.E. Triangle shows the answer to that very important question, "How do I avoid making bad relationship choices?" If we can see others realistically we can ENJOY them for what they are and not make them into what we want them to be. In other words, we operate **outside the F.A.D.E. triangle.**

Axiom - Trying to make relationships happen almost assures their eventual failure.

Finding the "right person" is a fallacy, usually meaning we are afraid of intimacy. It's simply not our job. Most of the couples I've met who appear to be happy were not actively seeking a partner when they found each other. They were able to see clearly as the liaison developed and did not force the relationship to conform to a preconceived idea or meet some magical need.

These highly successful relationships are dynamic and can grow and adapt as needs and conditions change. They don't result from idealizing other people. Those who have this calm state of mind are also more prepared for true intimacy. Even adolescents can learn to see beyond their romantic fantasies, but they need encouragement to think independently and to have accurate information about intimacy. They also need to be shown how to relax in social situations.

Thus, we cannot simply will ourselves into a satisfying relationship, but we can, by the choices we make, increase the odds of finding what we need. This brings us to another axiom:

Axiom – We are not likely to find healthy relationships in sick places.

People who are capable of (or in the right frame of mind for) honesty and intimacy are not likely to be found at parties, bars, nightclubs, or other places that operate on the basis of creating an "atmosphere." Such illusions of glamour and excitement belie the emptiness and lack of substance that prevails. Even social organizations, or church groups are not necessarily based on authenticity. With scrutiny, however, groups with the necessary elements can be found. If we pay careful attention, we can determine if honest sharing is taking place.

If we can't find a group that encourages openness and honesty we can create one. A few individuals in a town where I lived for a while started a singles discussion group. They divided attendees into rooms by topic. They tackled the tough questions like "How can you tell if a person is trustworthy?" or, "Should you have sex on the first date?" Perhaps the most interesting to me was, "What did you learn from your last relationship?"

Students or other young adults can start these highly candid groups. This type of honest sharing is called, "self-disclosure." How accurately someone reports about themselves is the best measure of their character. There are ways to make educated guesses about the people you meet. For example, the next time you're in (I hope) a relationship discussion group ask for a show of hands of those who never lied. If any of them raise their hand, then ask those people a follow-up question, "When was the last time you told the truth?"

It's useful to also listen for absolute statements in general. If people say they have never or would never do things that are common things to do, they may be intentionally lying, or they probably are not very self-aware. If you hear anything like the statements below, run as fast as you can.

"I never feel jealous."

"I never get angry."

"I am always respectful of women."

Of course, the best way to know someone is to observe them over a period of at least a few months. Seeing them in a variety of situations helps too. Remember, if it seems too good to be true in the very beginning, it probably is too good to be true. When we find their imperfections and love them anyway; that's real love.

Glue U.

When people are genuine, bonding can occur. Bonding can be described as the activation of chemistry, which creates an emotional and neurological link between two human beings. The chemistry involved in bonding is often confused with lust or purely physical attraction, but the difference is extremely important. Lust reacts to the object while bonding reacts to the whole person. Therefore, bonding can occur in any relationship whether romance or sex is involved or not.

Bonding may begin during the formation phase of a relationship but continues throughout. The strength and permanence of the bond depends on life circumstances and the compatibility of persons involved. Other factors, such as the kind of social support the couple enjoys, also affect the long-term potential.

Meeting people at places where atmosphere is created interferes with healthy bonding, because we are chemically altered by the "scene." Further, as I mentioned, we are also less likely to find a suitable partner if we are looking for one, because the act of seeking alters our perception. Paradoxically, if the individuals are fulfilled and functionally self-reliant before the relationship forms, a greater likelihood of an enduring, healthy bond exists.

We cannot force ourselves to bond with another person, nor can we force them to bond with us. Liking or being attracted to someone does not guarantee reciprocal feelings. Disinterested parties are no more in control of their disinterest than suitors are in control of their infatuation. The right stuff is either there or it isn't. To take such occurrences personally is not justified, but we often do. Remember, they're just rejecting you, the object, or their impression of you; they don't know you as a person.

Romance Languages

Today romance is mostly economically-driven and mythical. Romance and dualistic thinking about gender (seeing men and women as opposites) were more viable reasons for mate selection in an era where roles were specialized, and people occupied more (opposite) complementary roles once they married. In most modern relationships, however, it is more necessary to cooperate and collaborate than to have romance fueled by exaggerated gender differences.

In fact, romantic yearnings can rarely be mustered or satisfied when both parties are overworked, and they must play nice all day long in the workplace, raise families, etc. There is less room for wowing and wooing in the modern relationship. The expectation that a partner will always look their best and act their best is a setup for failed relationships.

Recently a twenty-year-old commented on an online forum that she doesn't celebrate Valentine's Day:

"I think it's an absurd idea that people should devote one day of the year to show someone you care about them. We should be caring about loved ones throughout the entire year."

I agree with her premise, although I don't object to others celebrating that way. The point is that romantic, symbolic gestures can't replace the need for everyday demonstrations of active love. We need less drama in today's world, not more.

Nonetheless, popular culture constantly feeds these expectations. Melodrama, especially the soap opera variety, and reality TV (and now our government, unfortunately) may have the most destructive effect. These characters teach that looking good and being passionate are much more important than behaving well. In these stories all is fair and expected in love, including cheating, lying, and even violence. This kind of entertainment reinforces the idea that sexual desire is out of control and dangerous and separates the rational self from the sexual self. For devotees of these genres' this can become drama-driven self-fulfilling prophecy. For others it can be a harmless escape. If you are drawn to this type of entertainment, it's a good idea to watch the watcher along with the program.

The seeds of destruction of many contemporary relationships are sown by winds of romantic courtship. Romance contributes to relationship and sexual violence because it creates a phase that sets up unrealistic expectations. When the magic of the early drama recedes, the tragic descent of civility begins. Overly romanticized relationships may eventually beget violence, or at least hostile indifference.

Often people fear that they will not find true love in the absence of romance. Some women have told me they want to be reminded how special they are in their primary relationship. Men often tell me they enjoy the excitement of the pursuit. Again, these ideas reinforce the notion that the affection of a woman is won by smooth deceit or manipulation.

For some men (generally believed to be more instrumental than women) flowers can mean I want something or did something. For some women flowers can mean I am worth something. If women allow men to define their value (or vice versa); they shouldn't be too surprised when they are depreciated and traded for something newer or "better." Their narcissism may allow them to feel good at times, but is doesn't render them secure in relationships.

Romance is a subtle form of social control over coupling, similar to those that existed in the past. A quiet revolution has taken place in American culture. In the first wave, during colonial America (and still in some subcultures today) young men and women were closely watched during the early phases of coupling. "Bundling" was a practice during this era, which involved a young woman and her suitor sleeping in the same bed with a board between them or him being wrapped in blankets. This was considered necessary because families often slept in a one room house together and space was limited. Suitors often had to travel long distances, so staying overnight was not unusual.

Later, dating began, but usually with chaperones. Eventually, young men and women dated without supervision. Currently, many young people are not dating in the traditional sense, but instead are "hanging out" or "hooking up." I see all of this as an unsurprising progression because the emphasis has shifted from external control to internal control. We trust our young people more and expect them to be responsible for their actions. No doubt the availability of birth control eased our minds too.

Modern youth are also beginning to differentiate more clearly between sex and friendship. Hanging out with opposite sex peers gives a strong message that males and females can be together, alone, and still control sexual impulses. The sense of urgency to define relationships is less strong than in traditional dating, which usually started out with boy-meets-girl assumptions. Hooking up, while not devoid of risk, at least invites clear communication.

One of my peers in college was a bit ahead of his time. He approached women frequently and simply asked if they were interested in "a brief and totally meaningless sexual encounter." Although this was perhaps a little too direct, at least his agenda was clear. We can help students today by teaching them to be more open in their efforts for relational fulfillment.

In summary, the best and longest lasting relationships result from staying relaxed and getting to know people over a period of time. We must manage our emotions and our expectations regarding what a relationship can realistically do for us. Establishing a clear identity, including sexual self-awareness, makes us ready for intimacy - not the other way around. We cannot find ourselves in someone else, but we can find ourselves, then someone else. Regarding relationships, an appropriate saying for modern times is, "If at first you don't succeed, stop trying so damned hard."

Thirteen - Getting In Sync

"The students realize that it's their life I'm talking about: it's out of balance, they're struggling to put it into balance. How are they going to do it?" - Robert McKee

The Asynchronous Development Model©

If sex and relationships follow an arduous path to maturity, we need to help youth prepare for the journey. Developmental education gives youth a heads up about the challenges they will face. It includes the idea that they may grow at different rates compared to peers. How much angst could be reduced if teens knew and accepted that how they look, or feel is normal and will change? Much suffering would be avoided if boys and girls were told that sex requires more than just the hardware; it requires the soft skills of self-awareness and communication. Knowing these things is like an emotional inoculation. It's also skills-training for reality-based love.

The main idea of **asynchrony** is that human development is normally uneven and individual. Each person develops at their own rate in several developmental areas. Therefore, an individual can be out of sync with peers, and can even be out of sync within themselves. Youth engage in what's called "social comparison" so they will see how peers seem to be and they may feel ahead or behind in some ways.

Most of us in the social sciences have been influenced by the great thinkers on human development: Freud, Erickson, Piaget, Kohlberg, to name a few superstars. They all have one thing in common; they see human development as unfolding in stages and define what is normal or typical for each stage. Positive results are determined by the level of conformity to these "normal" checkpoints or milestones.

This approach is sometimes referred to as the "nature" view because of the "natural" stages and less emphasis on environmental, "nurture" influences. While stages and milestones are helpful in comparing people to each other; they are limited when we try to examine the uniqueness and actual needs of individuals. If we adhere too strictly, we focus on what's normal instead of what's normal for THIS person at THIS time. We concern ourselves with the benchmarks that may tell us how far they need to go, but not what they need to overcome, or how much time they need to get there.

On the other hand, if we emphasize the environmental influences too much we ignore a key part of individual development. We might call it the internal environment - pressures from within that drive ideas and behavior. Understanding the asynchronous aspect of human development is a step in shifting the focus onto the individual and understanding the pressures they feel and the resulting behaviors.

As mentioned earlier, this concept of "asynchrony" means that people grow up at different rates. Some are ahead of their peers or classmates in some ways; and they may be behind in other ways at the same time. Of course, some are about average. Focusing on eight different developmental areas aids us to see how students or other youth view themselves and each other. These areas are:

Physical

Emotional

Cognitive

Academic

Social/Relational

Sexual

Moral/Ethical

Career

These eight principal areas (domains) and how to assess them will be discussed and amplified later but, for now, let's look at a few obvious examples of asynchrony.

Some students are more physically developed and mature earlier. Others mature later and look younger even though they are the same age. These differences matter because they can affect the experiences of youth. For example, research on early-maturing girls show they are more likely to associate with older boys and thus are exposed to alcohol, sex, etc. at a younger age. They may get into more situations they aren't ready for. Late maturing boys and girls may be victims of teasing or bullying or may become bullies to compensate or "prove" something.

Other students may be way ahead of their peers academically but may be behind socially. They may try social strategies that don't work and may worsen the situation. Sometimes being too far ahead of peers academically creates problems. How many students just don't fit in or "dummy down" and underperform academically to avoid standing out amongst their less gifted peers? I see this all the time when teaching. Bright students will clown around in class, so they don't set the bar too high and turn off other students.

Sometimes it's the opposite. One student in a class will answer virtually every question I ask, or they dominate group discussions to prove they are smart. Usually they are, but they don't detect the class's reaction to them. Academic skills are ahead of the group, but social skills are lagging.

In my entire teaching career, I only had to remove one student from my class. He had a degree and was going for a second degree. He dominated discussion so much that other students complained. I felt the need to confront this. Even though I did so carefully and privately, he became agitated and threatened me. He was ahead of his classmates academically by a wide margin, but emotionally and socially he lagged way behind. A four-year-old occupying an adult body can be a scary thing.

Asynchrony (or being out of balance) doesn't just apply when we compare ourselves to others, it can also mean we can be asynchronous within ourselves. Again, we can be ahead of ourselves in some ways and behind ourselves in other ways. This can be a factor in how youth put pressure on themselves to accelerate or slow down their progress. The mechanism for this is the "ego ideal" or, in other words, a different or better self we think we should be.

This adds to the pressures, and how we react to these pressures will determine whether we make good decisions or bad decisions. For example, a teen lacking in social competence may drink alcohol, even if they don't want to, so they can relax and feel more like they are part of the crowd.

So, these ideas; that human development is asynchronous, that we engage in social comparison, and we aspire to an ego ideal, are the keys to self-understanding which leads to making better choices. To do effective prevention work or any intervention/counseling work we need to start where the client or student is and that varies from individual to individual.

I once met with a mother and daughter after the mother called and expressed concern about her daughter failing her classes. During the interview the daughter said at least three times she had been having thoughts about hurting herself. The mother ignored (or just wasn't ready to hear) the comments. At that point I asked the student to leave the room and I posed this question to the mother, "Don't you think it would be a good idea for your daughter to decide she wants to live before we concern ourselves with her GPA?"

This student was depressed but mostly due to her situation. Looking at this distressed student through a developmental lens, she was not socially or emotionally ready for the stress of college, even though she had the cognitive and academic ability. We can assume there are other students who have similar profiles and, if they understood why they have difficulty coping, they could address this as a problem to be solved and skills to be learned as opposed to an external overwhelming force, psychiatric condition, or personal failure.

Every student probably has some asynchrony and though it may not be as serious as the example above, it is possible to see each person as an individual. From a developmental perspective we can assess the issues(s) with which each student is struggling when we have a way to understand their unique profile. The Asynchrony Model does this well and minimizes resistance because the model doesn't diagnose pathology or judge people. We set the tone by telling students that asynchrony is normal and everyone shows it at some point in their lives. Practically speaking, since we cannot usually assess every student on a campus, we can show them how to do it themselves individually or in groups.

Sample Group Presentation on Asynchrony

Section 1 - The General Asynchrony Scales

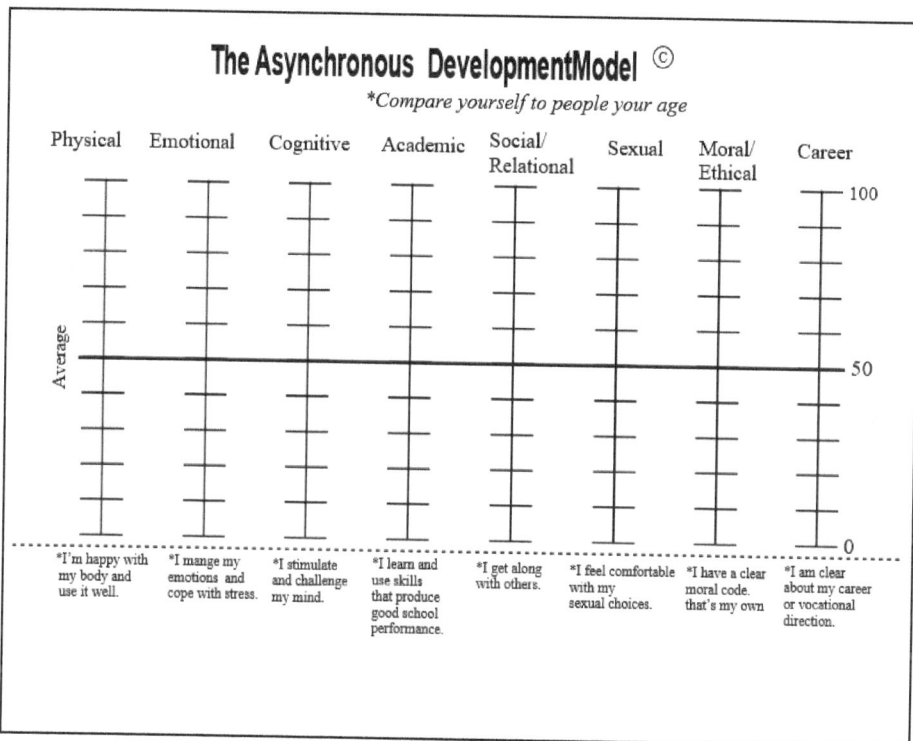

To use the general scales, we describe what they are and how to use them. We ask subjects to compare themselves to others in their cohort (age group) based on how competent they feel in each of the developmental areas.

The image above shows the General Scales and instructions on them. If you invite someone to do the profile stick to the descriptions on the general scales. That way everyone is getting the same instructions and that makes the data more useful and helps us establish norms in our research.

The general scales give us a rough idea how they see their development compared to same-age peers. Later, some subscales will give us a closer look at specific issues that affect their perceptions of themselves.

In the general scales we cover eight domains of development and invite students to plot their perceived level compared to peers for each domain. The scales range from a value of 1 to 100 and average is 50.

When you view the image of the scales above you'll notice that the general scale descriptions are somewhat vague. This is intentional because they are used as a practice exercise to learn how to do the ratings. They can also be used to find obvious discrepancies in ratings that may come later in the subscales. When they do the subscales, they will be rating more specific items like:

Physical: What is your overall sense of physical wellbeing in terms of health, maturity, athletics, and attractiveness? How well do you use what you have?

Emotional: Do you generally feel positive and are you coping with stress adequately?

Cognitive: Do you like to stimulate and challenge your mind by solving complex problems, puzzles, etc.?

Academic: Do you find yourself spending enough time doing your school work, whether it is reading, studying, or research, etc.? Do you have good skills in these areas?

Social: Are you making acquaintances and have some people you feel close to?

Sexual: Are you comfortable with your sexual beliefs and behavior? How well do they coincide?

Moral/Ethical: Do you have a clear moral code that reflects what you personally deeply believe?

Career: Are you satisfied with where you are in the career exploration process?

To keep it simple we ask them to compare themselves to what they think is typical for their age instead of expecting them to be developmental experts. The average is defined as what they believe is average or typical for their peers. It doesn't matter how accurate or objective they are at this point because we are interested in their view of themselves as they engage in social comparison. It's their perception that determines the level of pressure they feel.

Why this matters

When youth lack information about their asynchrony pattern, they feel pressure, and they will, Step Up, Catch Up, or Give Up. This means they will either: 1) develop appropriate goals to address the developmental asynchrony or, 2) take short cuts that may lead to poor or impulsive decisions, or 3) give up because of feeling hopeless. With information and increased self-awareness (plus support) they can gravitate more often to "Stepping Up."

One college student I worked with provides a good example of the most favorable response. This individual had severe deficits in social skills and extremely high levels of social anxiety. When we first met him, he was literally unable to carry on a phone conversation long enough to order a pizza. After involvement in our social skills group for less than a year his growth was remarkable. That same individual was, by then, starting as a Graduate Assistant and was teaching a Biology class at the university. How can such a profound change in such a short time be explained? With one word - Asynchrony!

His asynchrony was the problem AND the solution. He was seriously delayed socially, but very advanced cognitively. We simply capitalized on the fact that he was highly intelligent, and he could understand how much his social issues interfered with his clear career goal of becoming a Biology teacher. In this instance all we had to do was provide a safe space for him to practice social skills. We assigned him to a Social Skills group that was not just academic but included field trips. He went with the group to a restaurant and they were assigned the task of ordering their food, but also conversing with the restaurant staff to learn at least one interesting fact about them. We followed that with a river cruise and required them to sit by a stranger and start a conversation. This individual with the most profound limitations did well because he was a biology major and talked about the birds and vegetation along the riverbank. He used a strength to address a limitation.

For him to do that without the group would have been nearly impossible because he would have felt so much anxiety he would avoid it. The level of pressure influences the degree to which a thoughtful, organized response will occur, or a more impulsive reaction takes hold. We need a certain level of pressure to be motivated but too much pressure can affect performance.

The dilemma is how to increase pressure in some of the eight developmental areas and decrease it in others based on that person's dreams and goals. Overall, we want to balance the pressure or keep it at optimal levels. This is sort of like the tires on a vehicle. If they are low in pressure it impedes performance. If we increase the pressure a little, performance is better because of less resistance. Of course, we all know what happens to a tire under too much pressure.

The famous psychotherapist Alfred Adler said, "There is no such thing as talent. There is pressure." Aptitude makes a difference, but the argument about how much difference will never be settled and we're not going to try here. We do know, however, that those who achieve at a high level respond to pressure differently than those who don't. Sports fans know this from personal experience. Just recall the last time your favorite sports team was in a tight situation and the intense pressure you felt. Now imagine actually being in the game and feeling that tenfold. Could you perform under that kind of pressure? Many athletes say they thrive on it. Some admit they can't deal with it and give up on sports despite being extremely gifted athletes. For most of us the best answer is, "It depends on what the game is and how much we care about it." In other words, is the pressure on the side pushing us to do something stronger than the side pushing us not to?

There are spectators in this game too. At the high school level (college too) counselors and advisors should weigh the expectations of parents heavily and determine how much the students' goals are internalized vs. trying to please or appease parent-spectators. That way we get a better sense of the level of support students will need, or we can help them set goals more suited to them.

The challenge and art of counseling, mentoring, or teaching is learning when to try to decrease pressure and when to increase it.

Section 2 - The Subscales

The Physical Scales

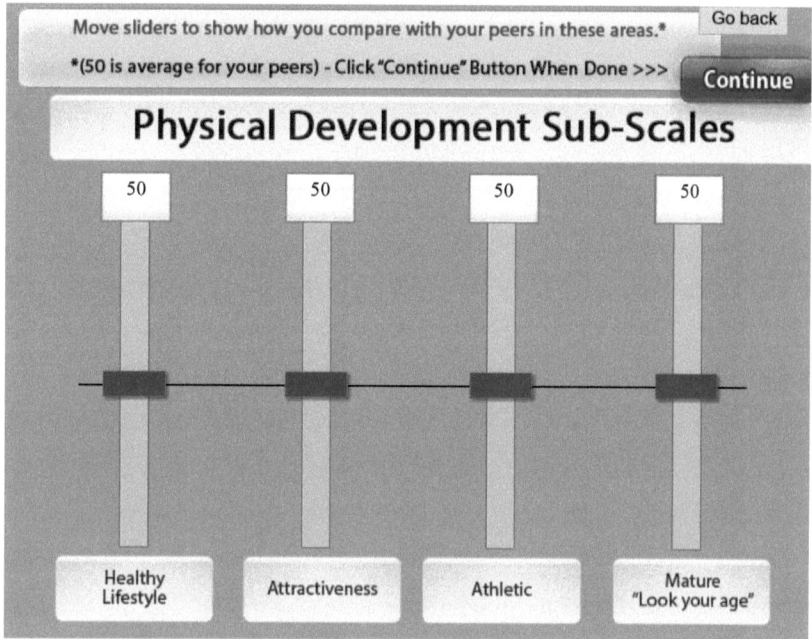

The Physical scales invite subjects to rate themselves on four sub-scales. The first is lifestyle related and gives us an idea how well the individuals are taking care of themselves. High or low ratings on this scale should be explored with the subject after all the scales in the entire set are completed.

The second item is about physical attractiveness. This is a sensitive issue, and studies show that this is the number one concern of youth across many cultures including the United States. Students may underrate this to look modest or may overrate this to hide sensitive feelings. This is not a problem because we have a baseline to compare the results. If their answer deviates a lot from this baseline we are concerned, and we provide an exercise in this area to help youth clarify what can be valued along with physical traits.

The third item is athletic. This may be an important issue for some and not others. This can be visited again, after the subject has completed the entire profile. It's especially important to examine whether they had athletic aspirations that are unfulfilled. There may be activities available on campus to address this.

The fourth item is about how mature they look for their age. This can profoundly affect their emotional or social development. Boys who look older than their peers tend to have more confidence. Girls who look older have some advantages and disadvantages. They may be exposed to things earlier than less-developed peers, but after adolescence they tend to be more confident. This could be because they survived some adversity and became stronger. The "mature for your age" should be followed up on if a student gives high or low scores on this. Attempting to see how this affects them can be helpful.

The Emotional Scales

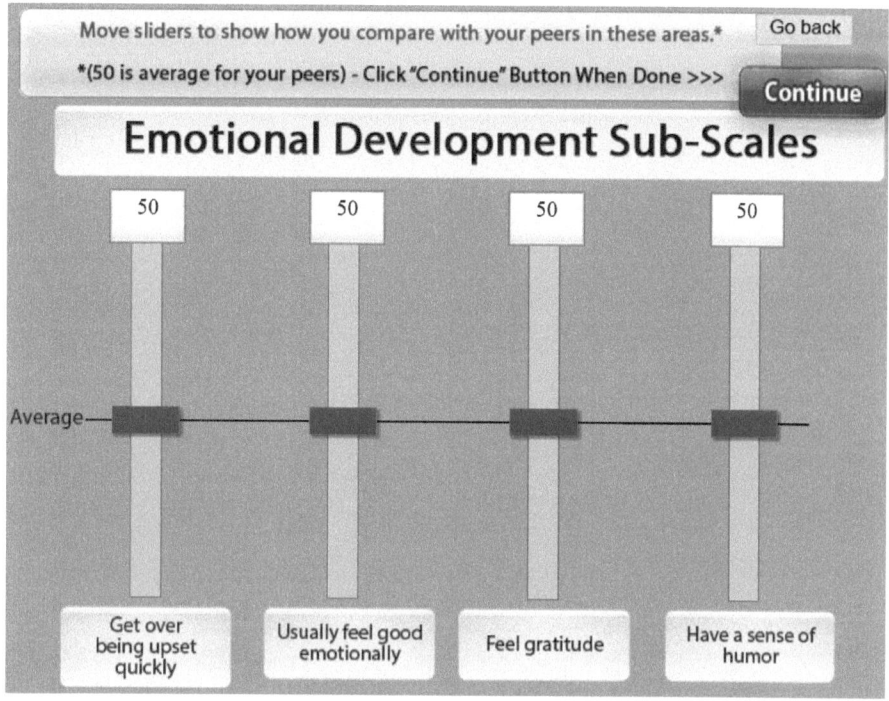

We cope with life better if we can express our emotions effectively and appropriately. This requires that we don't exaggerate or minimize the importance of events – keeping things in perspective. The abilities to feel gratitude, and to appreciate humor correlate highly with emotional stability. Counter-intuitively, we sometimes take actions to cope that are detrimental to ourselves and others if we get our feelings hurt. We may put salt in our own wounds.

This ineffective coping would include things like drinking or getting high to change our mood, or anything that we use to feel better - exercise, food, sex, music, entertainment; we could go on and on. The four emotional subscales help us see how well students perceive their ability to cope with adversity.

Students with low scores on these scales are at risk to act out, especially if they can't or won't discuss their feelings. The pressures of school can exacerbate emotional problems. Alcohol or drugs may provide temporary relief, but they become a substitute for more effective means of coping. They may be more susceptible to manipulation by others who try to make them feel better through flattery or worse through criticism.

The Cognitive Scales

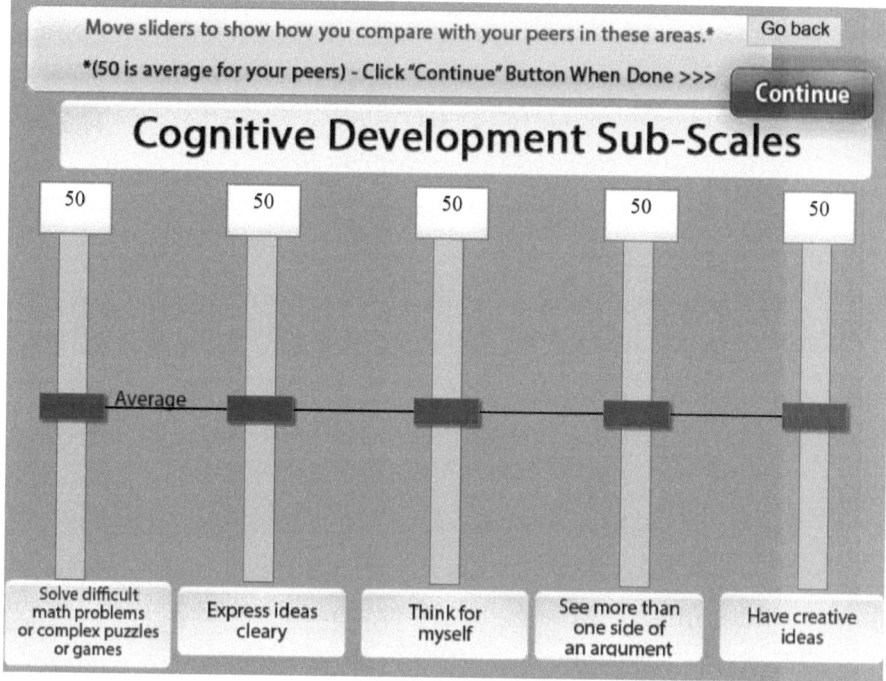

Cognitive development riddle:

I have two coins and they total 55 cents and one is not a nickel.

The riddle I just gave you is an example of something that requires cognitive skills. Don't worry if you don't have the answer right away, this is not a test and I'll tell you the answer at the end.

For our purposes cognitive means the ability to think in advanced ways to solve problems or come up with ideas. This involves abstract thinking which deals with concepts that are not real things. For example, a car is a real thing that is a form of transportation. Transportation is a more abstract idea because you can see a car, but you can't see "a transportation."

Cognitive functions also involve hypothetical thinking which means we can hold ideas in our heads and think of more than one possible implication or outcome. If so and so happens; then so and so might happen; or maybe something else might happen. You get the picture.

This includes the idea of critical thinking which involves testing ideas using the other two kinds of thinking to decide whether you agree with the ideas or not. That way we don't just accept everything without question. That's a pretty important thing in the type of society we live in.

Well, ok. What does all this mean when it comes to ratings?

If the subjects like complicated puzzles or games, or they like to solve difficult math problems they should rate themselves higher than average. If they like to think of new ideas or theories, they should do likewise. If they would rather just focus on real things and things they already know, then they should rate themselves lower. By the way, lower doesn't mean bad in this case, just different.

Students who are not less-developed cognitively may feel inferior or bored with school. They may be vulnerable to getting sidetracked into things in which they feel more competent. They may voluntarily engage in partying and sexual activities more than others to receive status or as a distraction. They may succumb to sexual pressure from others as a way to feel competent in something or feel valued. They may also succumb to academic cheating, especially if they're getting a lot of pressure from parents.

Answer to riddle: "One is not a nickel, but the other one is.

The Academic Scales

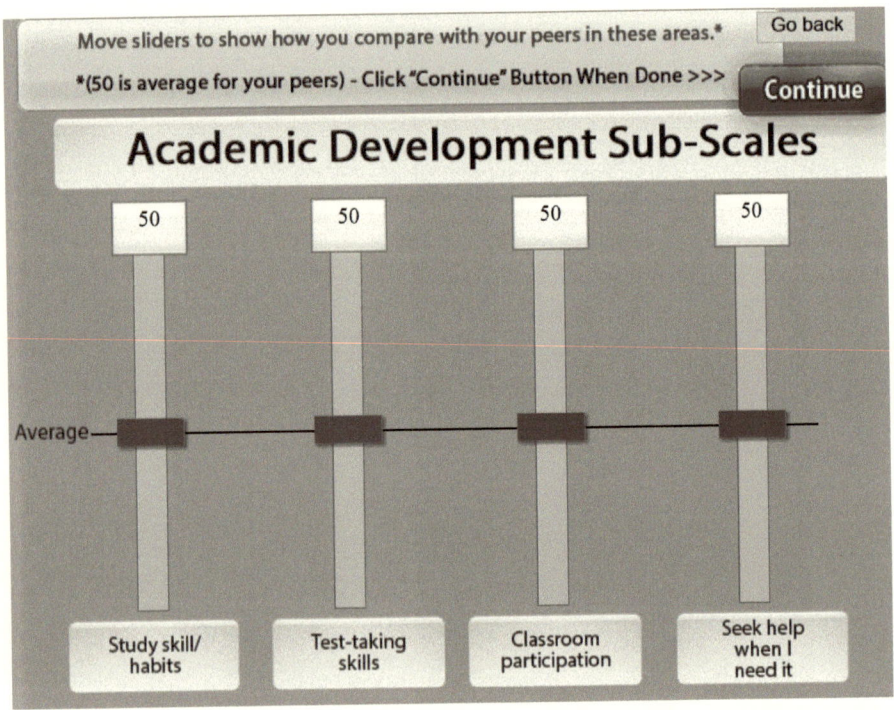

Academic Development...

One student told me:

"Study Smart, Not hard... That's what I kept hearing, but I HAD to study hard. Sure, I wanted to find more efficient ways of getting the job done, but I didn't think I had time to research how to do research. I was busting my brain trying to keep up with what I already had to do."

We realize that high school or college is not always a level playing field. Some students must be employed – even some full time, or they're athletes, or Greeks, and these things can take enormous amounts of time.

Some of them went to or are attending high schools that were/are not very demanding and college can be overwhelming for them.

Also, let's face it, some people are naturally more academically oriented, or have other advantages. Small changes can make a big difference. I'm reminded of a quote from Vincent Van Gogh:

"Great things are done by a series of small things brought together."

That really stuck with me and I hope it sticks with you because what you're doing right now may be that small thing that makes your version of greatness possible.

These academic subscales give us input on four areas of academic success; study skills, test-taking skills, classroom participation, and willingness to ask for help. Any improvement in these areas can have a snowballing effect because small successes bolster confidence and increase motivation. They also improve students' social resilience.

The Social/Relational Scales

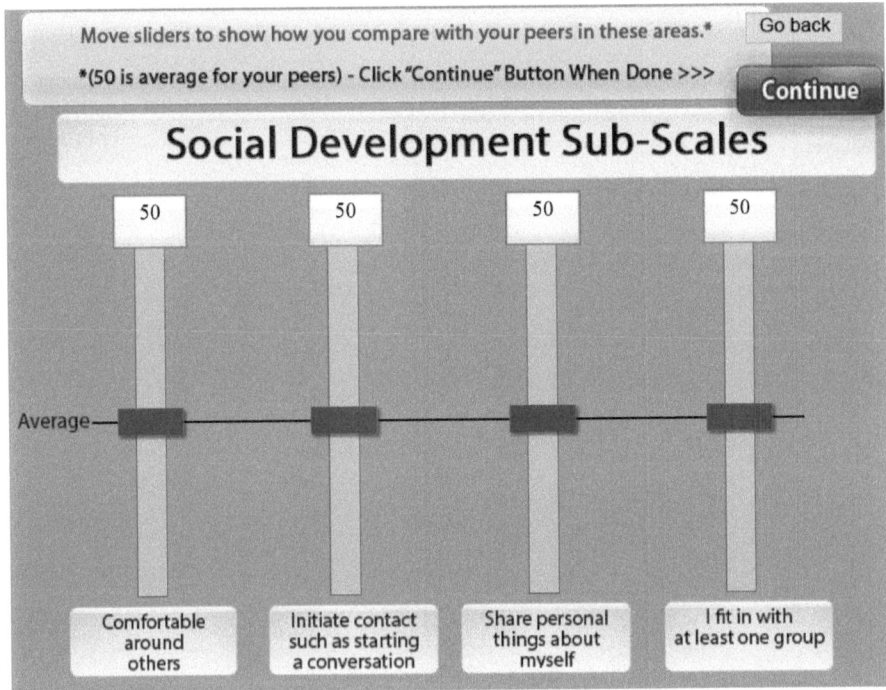

When we think about our social life we often dwell on what could be. This is normal because establishing and maintaining relationships, whether with acquaintances or our closest friends and loved ones, is an ongoing process. It can be very hard work or sometimes the most natural thing we do in life.

Making things even more complex, everyone has different social needs. Some people are so social they have to be around others almost constantly. Some like to keep to themselves more. It's important to remember that there's no normal when it comes to our relationships. Healthy is defined as whatever works for us as long as we can function in society and meet our life goals.

If a student socializes naturally this can be used to help them academically at times. Getting them involved in study groups may help. If they socialize too much they may need help in how to make solitary activity more productive. They may even need supervision. Some athletes are required to attend study sessions. This could be done with other students as well.

Sometimes students who are dependently social will reluctantly buy into the college sex scene and regret it later. One student told me she didn't want to have sex, but she feared she would not be invited to the parties if she didn't go along. We worked on her social skills, especially how to make friends in non-party social situations.

The Sexual Scales

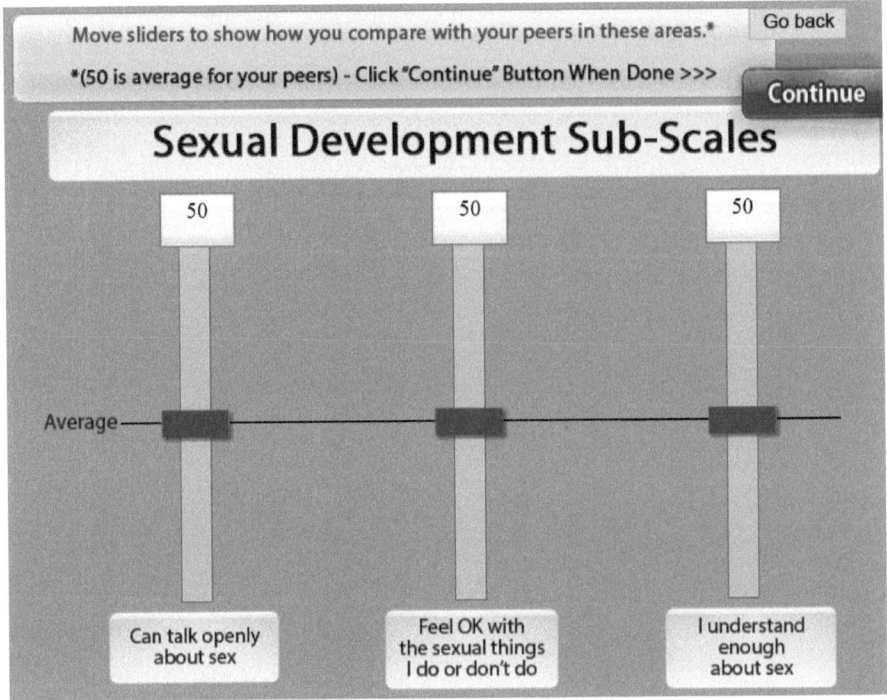

The sexual scales are designed to evaluate the students' attitudes and comfort level with sexuality in general. If they have a healthy perspective on sex they are usually less likely to act out. One complication is that people don't always admit their shame, so they may overrate themselves on these scales. When discussing sex with young people I often give them the following information in one form or another:

"Sex is neither good nor bad, but it IS complicated. It's a big decision to become sexually active and the important thing is to know what you're letting yourself in for. This starts with being realistic about what it will do for you. If you are concerned about performance, will sex prove you are a competent man or woman? If you believe it's connected to love, do you assume that everyone feels that way?

Of course, it's about being ready, but this means so many different things depending on how YOU define ready. For some it's a moral issue. For others a health issue. For many it is an important rite of passage and marker of adulthood. For those who want to feel grown up, "ready" may mean feeling heavy pressure to reach this milestone. It's the level of pressure WE worry about the most, because being pressured into something by ourselves - or by others - can lead to bad decisions."

Since we don't have "sex training" in our society we often have to figure it out as we go. It doesn't have to be that way. We can be a sexual being and be sensible at the same time. Everyone should develop a sexual strategy which might include planning for it, so we can do it well (in other words with enough knowledge to have realistic expectations) and thoughtfully; or it might involve planning how to avoid it until a later time when we feel truly ready.

Of course, some students are already sexually active, but it's never too late to evaluate how it's affecting their life and to adjust, if necessary. So, whether they have had sexual experiences with others or not, when they do this part of the self-assessment, they should answer the question. "Do I put too much emphasis on sex or am I avoiding dealing with it out of fear, or some other reason? Another possibility is that I'm doing it just right - or not doing it - and that's just right."

The Moral/Ethical Scales

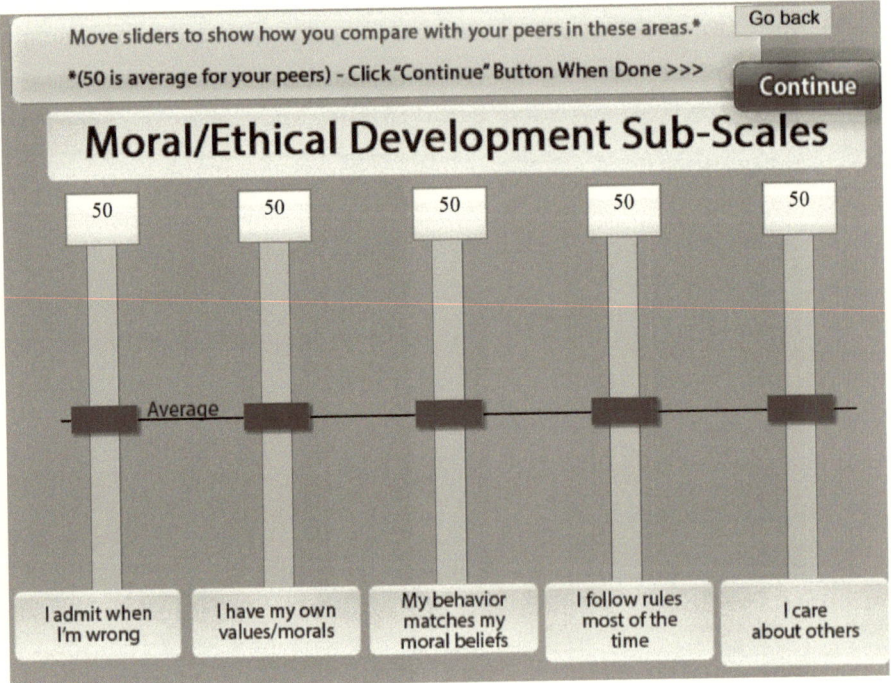

The highest level of morality is internalized personal morality. These subscales can be ranked accordingly:

"I follow rules" is the lowest level but important, if it's a good rule. If it's not a good or fair rule, we should try to get it changed.

Next is being able to admit "when we are wrong." We can't be moral without self-examination.

Third is "caring about others." Morality is pointless if we are not involved with anyone. Even if we are a hermit we still have to interact with nature or some living things.

Fourth is having "our own values" and not letting others decide for us. Internalization is the key to morality that will be always available to us. It's internalized morality that will enable us to say no despite the immediate social cost.

The highest level of morality is when our actions "match are beliefs." Assessing morality is complicated because moral thinking does not always coincide with moral behavior. Many people do things they believe are wrong because other developmental problems may interfere. For example, someone may feel strongly that stealing is wrong but may join others in doing it because they want to be socially accepted. Maybe, instead, they needed a challenge and the prized object was not easy to acquire. Those who are highly cognitively developed get bored sometimes. Too smart for their own good, but too empty to stop themselves from needing to get away with something. They can be sophisticated pranksters or criminal in their intent.

The Career Scales

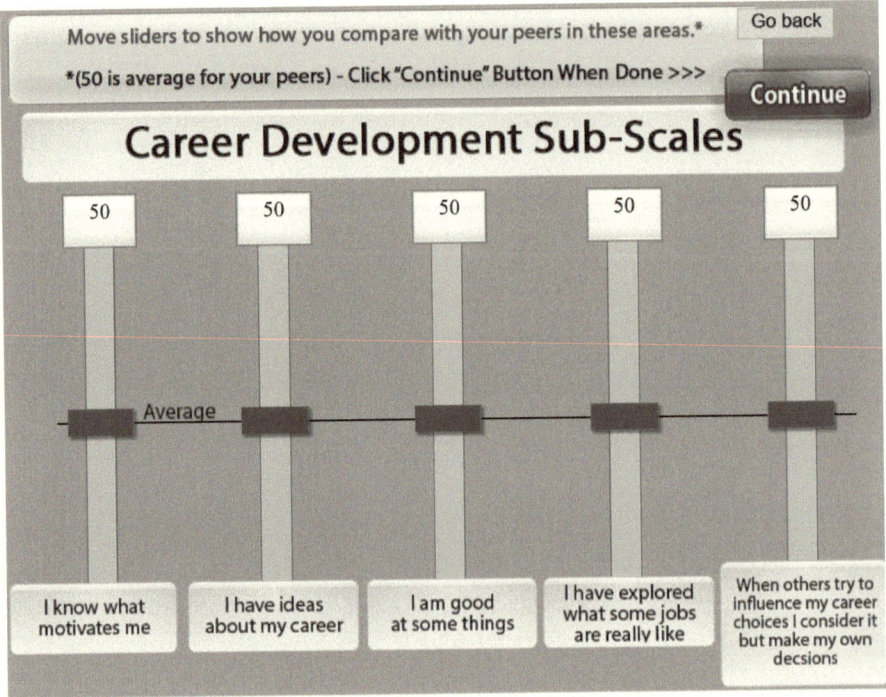

Depending on the age of the student, they will show different levels of progress in their career development. This is important in high school but not urgent. Ideally, by the time students are halfway through college they should be able to report at least average levels on all the items in this subscale. It's not necessarily a crisis if they don't, but it invites a discussion. If a student is in college without career direction, they may be more likely to focus on other areas and ignore academic goals. They aren't off track, they just never got on one.

Section 3 - Common Asynchrony Patterns and Implications

Specific patterns of asynchrony create different but sometimes predictable pressures. A student-athlete must emphasize fitness and skill development to excel in her sport. She usually has a demanding practice schedule. This takes time and energy away from other pursuits. She may suffer academically despite the special services she might receive as an athlete.

For the sake of discussion let's stipulate that this particular student has difficulty or is bored with academic tasks. Because of her athletic gifts she has never really had to make academics a priority. Nonetheless, she has to perform at a certain level to remain eligible to play sports and be able to have a career which may or may not be related to athletics.

This student probably feels intense pressure related to her classroom performance. She may have solid morals and ethics generally, but in this case, she may be tempted to cheat. For her, lectures about policies and ethics will not be enough. The problem must be addressed by either helping her find academic areas she is interested in or accommodating her learning style, or both.

Studies on cheating reveal that the power of the situation and opportunity are major factors in cheating. The peer effect also contributes. In a recent scandal at Harvard University almost half of an entire class was accused of cheating, involving 125 students. They virtually all rationalized with the "everyone is doing it" excuse. Seventy students were eventually suspended or expelled. This suggests that cheating is fairly common, even among our "best and brightest." Does this mean we should overlook cheating or lower our academic standards? No, we don't advocate that, but we do need to be more proactive with students who are vulnerable.

This might include those on athletic scholarships, students who have to work too many hours to pay for college, and first-generation students who don't have the family legacy of operating in academia. Also, all advisors need to be sensitive to the pressures their advisees feel. Thus, they need to understand the concept and assessment of asynchrony.

Let's look at another common pattern of asynchrony. In this case the student, Adam, has limited social skills and virtually no sexual experience. He is attending high school or college and hears lots of stories about the activities of others. He may feel intense pressure about being "inferior" or behind in his sexual and interpersonal development. Many "coming-of-age", popular movies highlight this theme, often chronicling the adventures of youth as they try to "lose their virginity." There are often high levels of comparison and competition to say the least.

So. Adam begins to make some awkward attempts at meeting girls and initiating sexual contact. After some failed attempts the frustration mounts. He looks around and sees other males who are "getting the women." They are not as nice or morally good as him and they don't even seem to really care about the women they're involved with. You know, "Nice guys finish last", etc.

Somewhere along the way this "good kid" discovers alcohol and finds the solution to his problem. After a few beers he is bolder and more confident and much less inhibited. Unfortunately, his judgment is now impaired as well. He could barely read social cues before but now we could say he's socially illiterate.

During an "asynchrony" workshop I asked some students to predict what would happen. Before I could finish my question, one spoke up and said, "Sexual aggression." This young man's profile is not uncommon on high school or college campuses and this is a problem we can and should anticipate. Further, this student is not the prototypical criminal rapist we are determined to weed out. He would never hurt anyone sober, but he may be dangerous when intoxicated. He may become a stalker if he thinks he's gotten some encouragement. He's an appropriate target for prevention because he is in serious need of developmental education and maybe more.

There are other students who act out sexually because they are morally behind in development, but socially astute. They use these skills to their advantage. They are difficult to help because they may believe things are going their way. They may not consider their effect on others until they suffer serious consequences themselves. If they have the cognitive ability to see the futility of maintaining the same behavior they may change, mostly because of self-interest.

The most difficult to address are those with low moral development and low cognitive development, but either extremely high or extremely low social development. They are either chronically careless womanizers (high social) in the first instance, or the violent rapists (low social) in the latter instance. The low social and moral types are dangerous because they are committed to what they do, and they lack a conscience.

A third type of asynchrony appears frequently on college campuses. Often there is a gap between moral and social/relational development. Moral development is high but social is low. The extreme example would be the street preacher who is highly focused on, even obsessed with morality, and shouts at passersby but never really relates to them. He often shows up on a college campus. He lumps all students into one category and condemns them to hell. Very efficient, but it's probably not conducive to converting them to his way of thinking.

This phenomenon shows up in more subtle ways for many students. They have come from strongly religious backgrounds and may feel uncomfortable with campus diversity and free thinking. They may do well if they find enough like-minded individuals for support and affiliation, but they may otherwise be overwhelmed, isolated, or vulnerable, or all-of-the-above.

I'm reminded of a friend who had strong religious ties and strong traditional family values. His daughter attended the school where he worked rather than move to a faraway campus. Within her family and familiar social network, she would be safe. She ended up pregnant in her sophomore year and soon after married, and left school. It's likely that she had strong social/relational and sexual needs that were outpacing the internalizing of her personal values. People with borrowed values are on borrowed time. If parents force values and beliefs on a child, then others can come along and persuade that child to think differently.

Overall, think of developmental imbalance this way. If different parts of us are highly asynchronous, reasonable compromise is difficult, if not impossible. We are at war with ourselves and we can't win without also losing.

Sample Asynchrony profile:

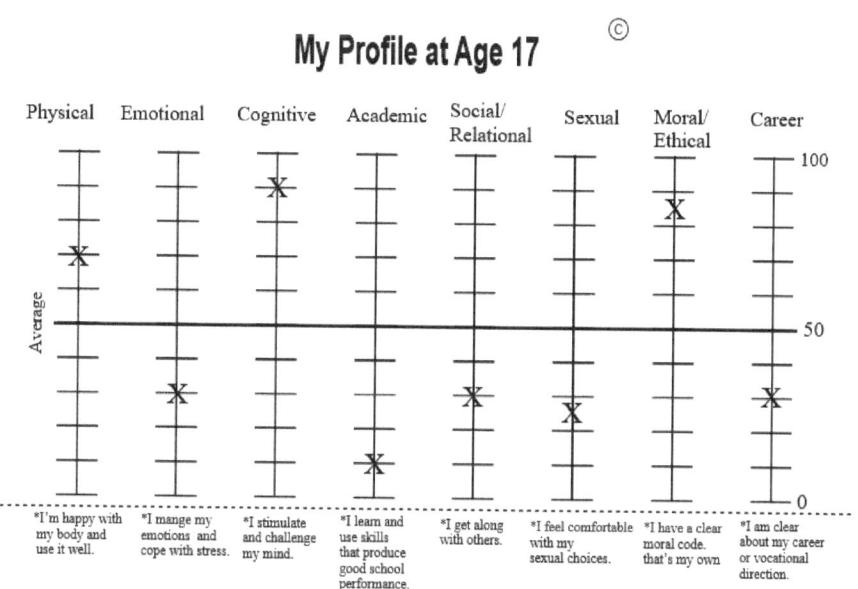

My Profile at Age 17 ©

At age seventeen I had a great deal of asynchrony. The x's on the vertical lines show morally (at least my moral reasoning) and cognitively I was ahead of my peers. Some of the other students called me the "Class Philosopher." Academically, I was way below average due to lack of motivation. I was a troublemaker in class because I valued intelligence but lacked the skills to achieve. I loved to argue to establish my intellectual bona fide. Emotionally, I suffered from mild depression and issues related to family problems. I eventually was seen as one of the "bad kids" because of the acting out while drinking.

Notice that the areas most out of sync are cognitive compared to academic, and social and sexual compared to moral. I treated people very well and actually focused on keeping my friends out of trouble. Once I would get drunk, however, I would make very clumsy attempts to engage girls in sexual behavior and I would sometimes become generally argumentative. This illustrates that we can have very high moral standards but not live up to them if we are emotionally compromised or substance-impaired.

NOTE: I suggested you estimate your own profile when you were a teen and compare it with how you are now. Try to figure out how your profile affected/affects your behavior and overall development.

Story Tellers

Another developmental concept associated with adolescence is the idea of the "personal fable." Adolescents often believe that they are unique and immune from the consequences of risky behavior. They adopt the "it will never happen to me" mindset. This may be rooted in a need to compensate for insecurity and fear of the unknown, but we don't help if we try scare tactics. These tactics don't work because they are based on half-truths, and we insult the intelligence of adolescents when we apply them.

We tell young people about the dangers of alcohol and drugs or the awful things that happen when they engage in sex. We ignore the fact that many have already conducted personal experiments and mostly found that nothing bad happened, and the experience was pleasurable. They conclude that our information cannot be trusted and that we just want to interfere with their fun. They tell their peers that their experience differs from our warnings.

Effective prevention tells the whole truth. Adolescents and young adults can hear both sides and make intelligent decisions. Virtually all cognitive developmental theorists state that older adolescents are capable of abstract and hypothetical thinking. Hence, we can tell them that drugs can really make them feel good and sex is incredibly pleasurable, and both can be fun, and we can tell them why. We can also talk about the risks. I sometimes use the analogy of jumping off a cliff into water. No doubt this is thrilling, but it's a good idea to know how deep the water is.

Generally - other than illegal activity or actions we are convinced threaten the campus community - it's not our business to tell students whether or not to engage in personal behaviors. Nonetheless, it is our responsibility to help them minimize the chances of negative consequences. We do that by doing what we're best at – education. But what should we include in the curriculum?

There are at least five elements to a solid college level sex education/violence prevention program. They are all related to fostering healthy development.

1)   Offer instruction on the developmental issues they face so they know what's happening to them. Teach them about asynchrony.

2)   Help students understand the effects of alcohol, drugs, and sex - both what they can do FOR them and what they can do TO them.

3)   Teach content about the joys of healthy relationships and intimacy, and what they need to learn to reach this level.

4)   Teach them about self-esteem and how to be aware of their individual vulnerabilities. If students have low or fluctuating self-esteem they will not be able or willing to pay the social cost of going against the crowd.

5) Show them how to develop a specific personal sexual identity and how to manage sexual behavior.

All of these elements should be implemented in a nonjudgmental manner and these services should be available to all students. It is preferable to offer them with males and females together to demonstrate that men and women can talk openly with each other.

Fourteen - Self Esteem and Sex

"Self-esteem comes quietly – like the truth." – Amity Gaige

Self-concept is related to a single domain and is fleeting. For example, in the physical domain, a new blemish or pimple may affect our momentary concept of self. We may feel self-conscious and believe that everyone is looking at us and that people actually care whether we have an imperfection or not. This all-eyes-are-upon-me, egocentric experience is called "imaginary audience."

Self-esteem is more global (broad and deep) than self-concept because it's influenced by several factors, not just what's happening at the moment. A student who has several areas of their lives that are going well will be less affected by a bad hair day or some other adolescent "crisis." If some students have only one way of feeling good about themselves, an issue that seems minor to us may be a true emergency for them.

We often encourage students to get involved on campus in several activities or organizations, but we also need to tell them why. Mainly, they will be less susceptible to negative influences and more likely to persist in their goals if they have high self-esteem produced by success in more than one area.

Athletes can be especially vulnerable because they often place all their bets on their sport. It takes extraordinary time and effort to compete at this level. If an athlete has a bad game, she may try to compensate by getting a quick ego fix. Imagine, then, if she has a career-ending injury or ineligibility for academic reasons. She will likely be temporarily without an identity and that is dangerous for her and the people around her.

Temporary loss of identity is an emergency for anyone, but especially adolescents and young adults because they have less history and momentum on their side. An adult has a reservoir of established patterns of behavior on tap and usually more patience.

A long-time colleague of mine, Dr. Ed Smith, occasionally reminded me that adolescents have a different perception of time as well. Adults know from experience that most things will resolve but it takes a while. To an adolescent "a while" feels like forever. Dr. Smith explains it as a function of the total amount of time we have lived, divided by a time increment, let's say a week. A forty-five-year-old has lived for about 2,340 weeks. A seventeen-year-old has lived for about 840 weeks. A week seems a lot longer if you've had only 840 of them rather than 2,340. The closer we are, the bigger things look.

People in the throes of an identity crisis usually react in one of two ways. They will either find a quick to achieve status and raise their self-concept or they will be assigned an identity by someone else. In the drug scene or the sex scene one can very easily establish oneself. You are connected the minute you get high or participate in sex. It's a lot quicker than attending public social events that require more complex social skills and patience.

Axiom - If you don't have a clear identity there is always someone willing to give you one.

Those in developmental crisis are very easy to manipulate. Cults are very good at recruiting this type of person. So are individuals who want to dominate their partners. Most students who dabble in drug abuse or unhealthy sexual relationships are not "bad" kids; they are developmentally challenged and are seeking an identity. For them, a negative or harmful identity is better than none.

"Liberty cannot be preserved without general knowledge among the people." – *John Adams*

The-above quote applies to democracy but also to the plight of young people in high school and college. Most students arrive on campus and they see new opportunities for freedom and innocent fun. Staff see that too, but they also see danger lurking. Ohio University is traumatized right now by having over a dozen sexual assaults reported in the first month of the school year. Students need to be warned of the danger but also why sexual assault happens. They may be more able to see it coming.

Freshman Orientation is the time to begin developmental instruction and sex education. Some of this can wait until later, but an intensive curriculum should be implemented as soon as possible. Warning them is not enough; we must also instruct them on the rudiments of healthy relationships and sexuality.

Providing a roadmap for what students can expect as adolescents and young adults is more necessary than in the past because so many students have less structure and supervision on college campuses. Many students live in apartment-style dorms, and/or co-ed dorms, and have less restrictive curfews, etc. More underclassmen have cars, and the internet has given them unprecedented access to social outlets as well as sexual opportunities and dangers. They need better internal controls and they are arriving on campus without them.

Some will be in almost constant contact with family and friends back home and this provides some support. Cell phones and social media keep them connected, but they are a mixed blessing because they also keep them dependent. Whether they are still tied to home or have separated cleanly, they need guidance to build a new nest, or at least partially leave the old one. They often don't realize how important this process is and many students falter. Much of the attrition in college is preventable if we do more on the front end.

The two main strategies for minimizing risks for young people are "cocooning" and "pre-arming." Cocooning means providing a deliberately designed protective environment. Some campuses can provide cocoon-like protection because they are staff intensive and culturally restricted, such as some religious institutions. They adopt the more traditional "in loco parentis" (college personnel as parent substitutes) approach.

Other colleges have less staff and more flexible rules, and they depend on students to be self-regulating. Pre-arming involves giving them the tools to avoid the pitfalls of matriculation by letting them know what to expect and giving them a chance to learn and practice the necessary skills. This includes how to monitor their self-esteem levels and realize when they are vulnerable. Each campus should assess its structural and cultural underpinnings and determine the kind of support students need to have a realistic chance of persisting to graduation without major disruptions. Once the staff, faculty, and students identify what their particular campus needs, they can develop more effective programming.

Let Me Entertain You

As any experienced student affairs staff will tell us, it's difficult to get and hold the attention of orientees. Therefore, programs that address developmental issues must be energetic, entertaining, and informative. The agenda should include elements of all five curriculum areas mentioned earlier in this book; instruction on specific developmental issues, the effects of alcohol/drugs and sex, the benefits of healthy relationships and what they look like, self-esteem, and how to manage their sexuality. Older students should be involved along with staff and self-assessment and learning tools should be made available to all students.

Another primary need is inoculation against an onslaught of products and ideas that promote hyper-masculinity and hyper-femininity. Gender (whether we consider it primarily a creation of God or of mankind) is the most commercially successful enterprise in history! Again, just imagine the amount of money spent on beauty and grooming products, fashion, romantic movies, modeling, etc. Images of hyper-femininity or hyper-masculinity surround us, ever reminding us that with a little more effort or a lot more cash we could be a player in the only game that matters; the quest for more power and/or more sex.

Our economy is vastly more dependent on these gender-aggrandizing products than foreign oil or any other commodity. Our financial markets would collapse almost instantly, if we decided that gender distinctions are a fiction, designed primarily to feed the voracious appetite of businesses. Since we are unlikely to change our culture to the point of nullifying these socio-economic effects, we need to help students to be wise consumers, not only of products, but also ideas. Self-esteem should not be so heavily reliant on how one thinks they look.

Sexy Education

The economic price tag of gender and sex, although substantial, is perhaps less than the emotional cost of all this hype. The broad spectrum of human sexuality becomes even more problematic because sexuality is exaggerated on both ends of the moral continuum. Those who favor Puritanical ideas and censorship see sex as something that must be suppressed and contained. They equate sex with unbridled passion and suggest it is impossible to control once arousal occurs, and all kinds of terrible consequences will result. Those who promote mainstream pornography portray sex as an amoral activity which is harmless. They try to instill the idea that sex is like an athletic event and some people are better at it than others. Indeed, just a form of adult sport. This inaccurate depiction causes people to feel inadequate.

One side takes sex too seriously, the other not seriously enough. These extreme positions feed into each other in that they converge to make intimacy impossible. Sex is not important vs. sex is everything – no in between! This splitting of sex and intimacy probably accounted for ninety percent of my counseling practice. Good (deeply enjoyable and comfortable) emotional closeness and sex involves interaction and clear communication between two people with realistic expectations. The material presented by the good guys and bad guys needs to be recognized for what it is, ad populist lore, or even propaganda.

The moralists emphasize all the bad outcomes and use scare tactics, while the pornographer emphasizes unrealistic good results, such as marathon sex with unlimited orgasms. Not surprisingly, many porn films use looping techniques and other deceptive editing to give the appearance that sexual intercourse is taking much longer than it really is. Actors, even the males, fake multiple orgasms, with a little cutting and pasting. Some movies of this genre, and folklore that supports misinformation, imply that the only way a woman can be satisfied by a man is through vaginal orgasms caused by penetration with a penis which is oversized and working overtime.

Even if students haven't been exposed to porn these myths find their way into mainstream media. Hence, young adults need information about the realities of sex, so they can know what is normative. Being uneducated only intensifies sexual hang-ups or compulsions. When people first start sexual experimentation, things can happen that increase anxiety or doubt such as him ejaculating "too quickly" or her "not being able" to have orgasms. Again, the sex industry thrives on feelings of inadequacy.

In reality, many females cannot have orgasms through intercourse alone because of anatomical differences, and sometimes for psychological or emotional reasons. For men, how long they maintain an erection is viewed as a measure of their manhood. These arbitrary measures of "sexiness" only tend to make people feel inadequate. Young people need to be taught to appreciate the wide range of individual differences within each sex and natural differences between men and women.

When I do sex education for college students, I always encourage them to celebrate the human sexual response cycle. Men tend to get aroused more quickly, reach climax sooner, and rapidly lose interest. Women tend to be slower to arousal, more likely to climax later, may have more orgasms, and remain interested in affection longer. If it were the opposite and women climaxed quickly and lost interest, we may not have survived as a species. She would pull away before impregnation could occur.

Causing people to question their sexual performance is unhealthy and promotes unrealistic and absurd ways to value sexuality. Many men are taking drugs, with some serious side effects, just to replicate this image of manliness. Some women fake orgasms to protect a partner's ego or their own. Many men and women think something is wrong with them because they can't enjoy sex as much as others. My next axiom provides clues for maintaining satisfying relationships:

Axiom - Most problems in relationships result from expecting too much or too little.

This applies to anything, from sex, to division of labor, to how much attention is doled out. Most couples start out a little disadvantaged on the realism scale. Since many families don't talk about sex openly and many parents are naïve or misinformed, young people enter the sexual arena (or even marriage), without the necessary information. So, we hear stories like this one from a young married woman who told me she went to a physician with a sexual problem:

"I went to the doctor because I wasn't having orgasms during intercourse. The doctor told me two things that sort of made sense at the time but later, I realized, destroyed my marriage. He told me that if my husband loved me enough he would make me have them by doing intercourse more vigorously. The doctor also said it would help if his penis was shaped like a mushroom."

It turns out she was extremely unlikely to reach orgasm. She expected her husband to do something for her she could barely do herself when she tried to masturbate. She told me she eventually left him to pursue the magic mushroom. But never found it.

Axiom - We are responsible for our own orgasms if we choose to have them.

Mutual orgasm is not necessary for reproduction, and the only real criterion for sexual maturity is the ability to reproduce. Only men must usually have orgasms during coitus to achieve continuation of the species, and even this – with advances in science – is unnecessary. Absent the desire to reproduce, both male and female orgasms are a matter of personal choice. In a loving relationship couples will try to help their partners reach orgasm, if they want them, and are able to have them. Nonetheless, doing so is optional. Sometimes love means honoring your partner's wishes not to have sex. We all come equipped with a do-it-yourself kit, so what's the problem? We can even take ourselves out to dinner first if we like.

Higher Education

Good, pleasurable sex is not merely a question of hardware; it's also a question of software. Clear and honest communication results in the most gratifying sexual experiences, if we define it as enjoying emotional closeness and physical pleasure. We cannot fully determine what our partners need or like unless we ask them, and they tell us. Sexual problems can be overcome with openness and creativity, and there are multiple ways to achieve orgasm, if this is determined to be essential to the relationship. In cases where orgasm cannot be achieved, couples can learn to cope. An adage I heard growing up was, "It's not what you have it's how you use it." A more instructive version might be, "It's not what you have; it's how well you know yourself and the person you're using it with."

Gender stereotypes also contribute to frustration and limit the ability of couples to satisfy each other's needs. If we believe that men are supposed to enjoy only certain kinds of stimulation and women are confined to other kinds of sexual expression, we inhibit a wide range of behaviors that could enhance relationships. Many relationships suffer because of the drudgery of sex by the numbers. A little behavioral latitude might reduce pressure to perform on cue and on script. Individuals who have preconceived ideas about sex become more frustrated since they experiment within a small radius of pleasure. Frustration can turn into anger and compulsion.

For example, both men and women can enjoy oral or anal sexual stimulation. Anatomically speaking, nerve endings don't discriminate. When I was in the military, some of the career soldiers talked about their experiences overseas. Highly skilled prostitutes knew methods of oral and anal play to enhance enjoyment for their clients. These military men were conventional thinkers and clearly heterosexual. I want to make it clear that I'm not advocating any specific practices; rather I'm suggesting that more people can be open about their interests, and not hide their desires or behavior from partners. There is less reason to feel ashamed or stray if these issues can be discussed without judgment. Even if the partner doesn't want to accommodate the request, the conversation itself is cathartic. It's not wrong to merely want something. Affirmation and acceptance weaken shame.

Even if the partner consents to behaviors outside the bounds of conventional practices, the interest in the activity may subside on its own. Sometimes people just want to try new things for the novelty of it. Other times couples expand their repertoire and continue to enjoy these things together.

Sexual experimentation is not inherently damaging. I remember the experiences of my youth that increased my own curiosity and knowledge about sex. Some of the aforementioned soldiers carried photos of naked women from far away, mysterious places, adding to the exotic quality of these manly storytelling rituals. Even before that, as a teen my curiosity had been piqued. Between my uncle's well stocked library of "skin" magazines and the erotic deck of playing cards my friend discovered in his father's dresser drawer, my visual appetite was whetted.

After seeking sexual variety with women as a young man, I eventually developed to the point I valued relationships more than sex or romance. I don't think I would have as much contentment today, though, if I hadn't sewn some "wild oats" in my youth. Perhaps everyone should have some adventures before they reach maturity. Some Amish groups - often viewed as conservative to the extreme - promote a period of "Rumspringa," allowing youth to engage in "English" behaviors such as drinking, pre-marital sex, etc. If it's going to happen naturally, why not acknowledge it and give it less power?

I had a close friend who died about ten years ago who hadn't experimented in her youth. She was the type of person who always followed the rules and did what people expected of her. She shared with me, a few weeks before she succumbed, that her only regret was never "taking a walk on the wild side." I wasn't sure what to say because I had done so; it wasn't anything like I expected, and it was nothing compared to having a close family and a peaceful life. I told her that maybe heaven for her would be like a song lyric I once heard containing the lament, "I wish I could have just one night with no consequences." She smiled and said, "I hope it's a long one."

I think the above examples show that sexual tolerance and experimentation will not necessarily permanently corrupt us. Also, we won't always be happy if we conform to unyielding social constraints. If our culture exhibited more openness and sophistication about sex, we could establish a code that places responsibility on each person to own and articulate what they want and to respect the rights of others.

We need to stop condemning people just for making their wishes known and, especially, for just having them. We also need to reward self-awareness and honesty. Sex can still be private but doesn't have to be buried deep underground, like radioactive waste capable of destroying us with every exposure.

Mythology 101

Things go wrong when we exaggerate the power of sex or perpetuate sexual mythology. Relationship or acquaintance rape results in part from the false beliefs that sex is something men need, and women don't, and it's up to the male to make sex happen. This type of blind belief sets the stage to see sexual misconduct as a normal behavior for males.

Other urban legends and folklore about men help lower the expectations society places on them. A female colleague told me a perennial joke about men, which illustrates how they are viewed. She described the male equivalent of PMS that plagues men every month, called SRH or "Sperm Retention Headache." There are many other jokes and stories that suggest men are controlled by their sex drive. This idea is countered by my next axiom:

Axiom - People can be aroused and think at the same time.

My previously mentioned colleague, Dr. Ed Smith, sometimes uses this story when he's doing work with men:

"Imagine you are in a bar and you meet a gorgeous woman and she takes you home with her and leads you to her upstairs bedroom, undresses and asks you to make love to her. You are passionately embraced and fully aroused when you hear a sound downstairs. She panics and says, 'Oh, I'll bet that's my husband, they must have let him out of prison early.' Do you think you would be able to stop?"

Sometimes students say that some men just have stronger sex drives, and this explains the aggression. They need to hear that men who aggressively pursue women may not have stronger sex drives than other males or females; they may just have more control issues. The sex offender is more likely seeking power over something abstract – such as the perceived power of women over him. He feels defenseless and opts for a preemptive strike. He might be convinced by his culture that sex with another willing or unwilling partner is necessary to affirm his "manhood," or he takes what he believes he deserves. Perhaps he strikes back, in a deranged way, at those whom he believes injured him.

Similarly, in a warped view of justice, some people take another's property by rationalizing the basic injustice of an economic system. Even otherwise honest people will sometimes cheat when they feel they have an unfair disadvantage. The difference between some acquaintance offender (where violence is not used) and the overtly criminal rapist is that the former is less aggressive and less likely to have a general criminal mentality.

The offender would not say that rape is acceptable behavior, but the rapist believes in what he's doing, or at least is beyond considering the moral question. Some acquaintance violators are socially marginalized individuals, who may have a culturally induced condition, and is also a victim. He is not necessarily someone who consciously and deliberately hurts another person.

The diagram below illustrates the potential for different types of sexual behaviors and the degree to which intentionality and compulsion play a role:

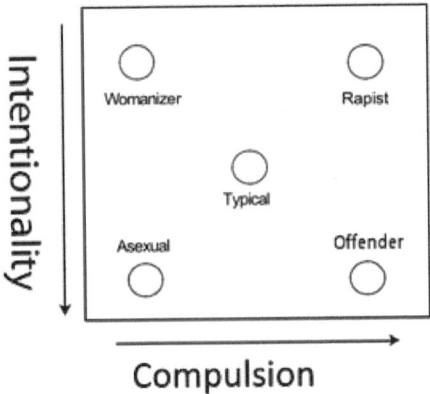

The Womanizer – (High intentionality, low compulsion). Seeks sex with multiple partners but is controlled and methodical. Is unlikely to rape or be accused of rape because he patiently waits for consent.

The Asexual – (Low intentionality, low compulsion). Has little interest in sex, so has virtually no intention or compulsion.

The Offender – (Low intentionality, high compulsion). He or she has a neurotic need for sex that will override cues from victims in some circumstances. This person does not premeditate or plan. May be a candidate for successful treatment, or other non-legal interventions. They may learn from their mistakes.

The Rapist – (High intentionality, high compulsion). Plans actions and is driven by intense compulsion. Cannot control behavior and is not likely to respond to treatment. Society needs protection from these types.

The Typical – (Moderate intentionality and compulsion). Notices cues and stops when partner gives clear indication. May be persistent in asking; but is not manipulative or aggressive.

Unfortunately, the offender and the rapist are often lumped into the same category. This is not appropriate or effective since one has a criminal mentality and the other does not. The offender is acting out his or her sexual neurosis or complying with a social or cultural script and is not fully aware that a rape is occurring. The rapist is a sociopath who is unlikely to care how his actions are defined and doesn't want to change them.

NOTE: I don't expect universal agreement on this Sexual Assault Potential diagram, but it is an invitation for men and women to use it as a discussion device.

Of course, offenders are still responsible for their actions, but these acts do not necessarily rise to the threshold of criminal misconduct. Criminal charges should always remain an option but, as I mentioned earlier, victims should have a say in the matter. Offenders have violated another person and should, at the very least, be civilly accountable and have a moral obligation to prevent future offenses, once they are educated about what they have done.

Check Your Baggage

Along with the baggage the offender carries into the encounter, the open and honest negotiation for sex necessary to prevent acquaintance rape is missing. When participants lack the social wherewithal to own and articulate sexual decisions, they could violate others.

If we look at it objectively, the vast majority of men have committed sexual assaults. A very common "lovemaking" scenario includes him touching her without asking permission. If he touches her in any "private" area he has technically violated her. She may say no and push his hand away, but the assault has already occurred! We have made sexual assault the norm in our culture by not requiring detailed conversation before sexual overtures are carried out. A conversation about a mutually agreed upon sexual activity that would avoid violation would go something like this:

He: "May I touch them?"

She: 'Yes, go ahead but that's as far as I want to go."

Notice that he has asked permission, and she has been clear about the limits. The conversation may be less formal, if the meaning is clearly understood, but if in doubt, ask.

Another cultural complication exists because men are encouraged to separate feelings from sex while women are more constrained to see sex in the context of relationships. These dynamics contribute to the tactics of men and woman as they leverage their attractiveness to one another. Men want to appear confident but not overbearing, and women want to appear coy but not "easy."

Whether or not men and women are naturally different in this respect, women who adopt this guise are apt to place themselves in jeopardy by "hooking up" with men who may make sexual decisions for them. Often these men are attractive because they appear self-assured. Women may be drawn to them, gravitating to the physical appearance or personality traits of these "players." That doesn't mean the victim is to blame, it just means some women may be more vulnerable because of this tendency.

One young man who had a reputation as a playboy told me he was providing a valuable service to women because "they would grow stronger when he used them and left them." This lover extraordinaire has convinced himself that his attractiveness is just his good luck, and there is nothing wrong with developing a God-given talent. This would be true if no deception was involved. Unfortunately, he broke a few hearts and eventually had a knife wielding jealous boyfriend almost make him pay with his life. Others were hurt as well, because the boyfriend's revenge was taken out on some other friends, who had slashed tires as a reminder of this Casanova's irresistible charm.

Sex without empathy, while pleasurable, is mechanical and empty. Men capable of empathy can't enjoy exploiting others and therefore have fewer opportunities for self-gratification, but they have a much better chance at knowing love. In John Laroche's movie, "Adaptation" a character profoundly says, "You are what you love, not what loves you." Being adored by "desirable" women can feel good, but not as good as feeling love for a whole person. This may be the most valuable lesson of my entire life.

Some women contribute to their own objectification. Women who do not accept themselves wholly and place inordinate emphasis on their looks, deep down, are never good enough. These "perfect," and artificial, women are the "Helens of Troy" in a sex war. Men fight over them because they can parade their manhood, just by being seen with these beauties. Some men eventually discover that the "sexiness" of these women is a mirage which evaporates on contact.

I've treated women who would never leave their homes without makeup. One told me she would "call in sick" on windy days lest people see her with messy hair. These women must conceal their imperfections and inner selves because they are alienated from, or unfamiliar with, some aspects of their identities. For women with low self-esteem, it is better to be admired than known. Men who want them to be "real" will never be appreciated.

Thus, predictably, these women are drawn to partners who can manipulate them by withholding admiration, and who won't pressure them to self-disclose. I heard the expression, "Play it cool" throughout my youth. This often-discussed "principle of least interest" means that the individual with the lower level of interest has the most power in the relationship and can exploit their partner. Meanwhile the "lesser" half can only chase a dream. Tragically, men and women who are real and reachable are often ignored or devalued. Where are the winners in these scenarios?

Real love takes time and we must love ourselves or we will not be able to wait it out. In their song, "Eleanor Rigby," The Beatles raised the right question:

"All the lonely people. Where do they all belong?"

The answer was provided in a later song by Crosby, Stills, Nash, and Young:

"If you can't be with the one you love, love the one you're with."

I would add, "Even if it's just you!"

Chapter Fourteen - Self Esteem and Sex

Epilogue

"Being a successful person is not necessarily defined by what you have achieved, but by what you have overcome." - Fannie Flagg

It turns out that being a good person is the same thing as being a successful person. It requires self-reflection, perspective, humility, and courage.

I have tried to be honest and objective in this book. I consciously took the risk of disclosing things about myself that are sensitive. As a professional person I felt it was important to wait until I felt ready to tell my story, lest it be misunderstood. It's also very difficult to write an autobiographical work when you're not famous. I had to constantly fight the worry that my story was not universal enough. Even though I've talked about private things with thousands of people, I still have to make educated guesses about what normal is. Perhaps my experience as a psychotherapist has skewed my idea of "normal" and I've overestimated the degree to which people will relate to this book. Nonetheless, I suspect many will relate to some of the experiences and I hope they will contact me to affirm this.

Some readers will experience resistance to my ideas, especially those who benefit from the status quo and believe they only need to make minor adjustments to appear avant-garde. This book, like my earlier one, is also not about polishing a few slightly rough edges of the present; it's about grinding away deeply ingrained ideas of the past. In some cases, I have suggested we abandon conventional ideas about sex and romance altogether.

I believe we must take the risk of self-disclosure if we are ever going to heal and help others heal. I strongly believe that men and women need to understand each other better and learn to share their humanity. Being mysterious or manipulative only makes us feel lonely and alienated. Sticking to a conventional role is sometimes comfortable, but it can be anti-intimacy. The rules for opposite-sex couples, or any other relationship are the same, "Tell the truth, never hurt your partner intentionally, and try to accept people as they are - until you can't."

You may ask, "How can I be truthful and not hurt people sometimes?" The answer is, "Look at your motive." Truth can be a weapon or a gift, depending on what you are trying to achieve. You must trust your motives to do any good in the world.

You might also ask, "How can we accept people as they are?" It's easy, if you accept that they are just like you, trying their best despite their shame. We only judge others' shortcomings when we are painfully aware of our own flaws, real or imagined. Everything wrong we do, we do for a reason. The trick is figuring out what the reason is and eliminating the need to do it again.

Lastly, some final words about sex. Sometimes I have cursed God, or fate (or whatever forces of nature) for sex being so wonderful, so spellbinding, and yet so damned complicated. It's frustrating that something this beautiful can hurt people, but it occurs to me that it has to be that way. If there were no complications, we would do it too much and we couldn't enjoy any kind of social order. We would be like horses or some other animals which sometimes eat so much they make themselves sick or they die. Conversely, without agonizing lust, we would avoid the complications of sex altogether and we wouldn't reproduce enough for the species to survive.

Some of my anecdotes may have sounded a little like bragging or glamorizing my past misdeeds. I want to make it clear that, although I had some adventures, I was miserable most of the time and none of the experiences were satisfying enough to make up for the misery. It turns out, however, that there IS a perfect sexual experience, but it's not solely based on an eroticism scale. When we can be physically, emotionally, and mentally engaged at the same time, we are fully present. This can happen in more than one way and I hope it happens to you. There are two experiences I think about from time to time that involved being totally free to be myself during sex, without losing the connection and passion. My partner has given permission for me to share these.

One of them happened after a difficult day at work. I had a boss who drove me crazy and he did some things that day that infuriated me. Later that evening my partner and I had sex and I was still angry. The sex was more vigorous than usual, but I was very focused on her nonetheless. When we finished we were both lying there with big grins on our faces. I told her, "You can thank that son of a bitch at the office for that one!" She asked herself aloud, "Let me see, what could I write on the card?"

The other time was earlier in our relationship. We were having sex and one of us said something funny and we both started laughing. We kept going at it and we kept laughing. We just didn't want to stop doing either because they both felt so good. It was an unusual experience for me, but it felt great to be so relaxed. Sex doesn't have to be so dire when you feel safe and you love someone.

Shame despises love and laughter.

About the Author

Tom Bissonette has over thirty years of experience in the mental health field, doing relationship work, teaching adolescent and young adult development, and preventing and treating addictions. He has been faculty at the University of Tennessee at Chattanooga since 1993 and was a counselor there until 2009. Tom received undergraduate degrees in English and Political Science from Saginaw Valley State University and earned a master's degree in Social Work from the University of Michigan. He is a proud survivor of the wild exploits of his childhood and his twenties. He is married and has four adult children and three grandchildren.

Although technically retired, Tom still does training, teaching, and consulting. He is delaying full retirement because there is still too much work on social justice to be done.